D1025599

Radical Peace

People Refusing War

William T. Hathaway

Published by:
Trine Day LLC
PO Box 577
Walterville, OR 97489
1-800-556-2012
www.TrineDay.com
publisher@TrineDay.net

Library of Congress Control Number: 2010923363

Hathaway, William T.
Radical Peace: People Refusing War—1st ed.
p. cm. (acid-free paper)
.
(ISBN-13) 978-0979988691 (ISBN-10) 0979988691
1. Peace—History—Literary collections. 2. Peace movements—History—Literary collections. 3. United States—Military policy. I. Hathaway, William T. II. Title

FIRST EDITION
10 9 8 7 6 5 4 3 2 1

Printed in the USA
Distribution to the Trade by:
Independent Publishers Group (IPG)
814 North Franklin Street
Chicago, Illinois 60610
312.337.074
www.ipgbook.com

Publisher's Foreword

Peace is costly but it is worth the expense.

—African Proverb

Abandon all attachment to the results of action and attain peace.

—Krishna

All we are saying is give peace a chance.

If everyone demanded peace instead of another television set, then there'd be peace.

If someone thinks that love and peace is a cliche that must have been left behind in the Sixties, that's his problem. Love and peace are eternal.

—John Lennon

One cannot simultaneously prepare for war and create peace.

—Anon

An eye for an eye only ends up making the whole world blind.

If we are to teach real peace in this world, and if we are to carry on a real war against war, we shall have to begin with the children.

Peace is its own reward.

Non-violence is the greatest force at the disposal of mankind. It is mightier than the mightiest weapon of destruction devised by the ingenuity of man.

—Mohandas Gandhi

There was never a good war or a bad peace.

—Benjamin Franklin

I like to believe that people in the long run are going to do more to promote peace than our governments. Indeed, I think that people want peace so much that one of these days governments had better get out of the way and let them have it.

—Dwight D. Eisenhower

Peace is a daily, a weekly, a monthly process, gradually changing opinions, slowly eroding old barriers, quietly building new structures.

—John Fitzgerald Kennedy

In peace the sons bury their fathers, but in war the fathers bury their sons.

—Croesus

One of the most persistent ambiguities that we face is that everybody talks about peace as a goal. However, it does not take sharpest-eyed sophistication to discern that while everybody talks about peace, peace has become practically nobody's business among the power-wielders. Many men cry Peace! Peace! but they refuse to do the things that make for peace.

—Martin Luther King, Jr.

Peace has to be created, in order to be maintained. It is the product of Faith, Strength, Energy, Will, Sympathy, Justice, Imagination, and the triumph of principle. It will never be achieved by passivity and quietism.

—Dorothy Thompson

Naturally the common people don't want war.... That is understood. But after all, it is the leaders of the country who determine policy, and it is always a simple matter to drag the people along, whether it is a democracy, or a fascist dictatorship, or a parliament, or a communist dictatorship. Voice or no voice, the people can always be brought to the bidding of the leaders. That is easy. All you have to do is to tell them they are being attacked, and denounce the pacifists for lack of patriotism and exposing the country to danger. It works the same in any country.

—Hermann Goering

You can't shake hands with a clenched fist.

—Indira Gandhi

Peace is not something you wish for; It's something you make, Something you do, Something you are, And something you give away.

—Robert Fulghum

Peace be with you.

—Genesis 43:23

Blessed are the peacemakers: for they shall be called the children of God.

—Matthew 5:9

Onward to the utmost of futures!
Peace,
Kris Millegan
March 19, 2010

For Daniela Rommel and Bob Schuster

Our thanks to Jim Karpen, Michaela Röll, Nora Boeckl, Jessica Strike, Friederike Jörke, Kris Millegan, Russ Becker, Kent Goodman, Ed Bishop, Bob Oates, Keith Wallace, Jay Marcus, Anna-Maria Petricelli, Lisa Hayden Espenschade, and Brad Booke.

Table of Contents

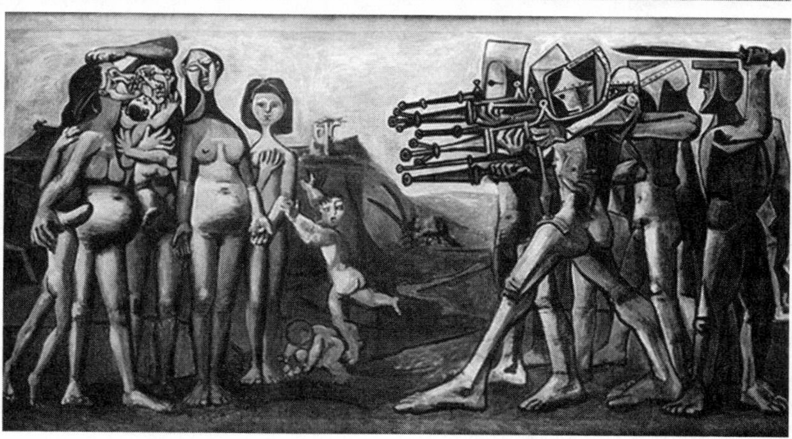

Introduction

They have healed the brokenness of my people superficially, saying, 'Peace, peace.' But there is no peace.

Jeremiah 8:11

When the prophet Jeremiah wrote those words, he could have been describing the public-relations strategy of the current US government. Barack Obama won the presidency and the hearts of billions around the world by pledging to bring peace. His humanitarian rhetoric promised a new era in American foreign policy, away from armed confrontation and towards cooperation. But since taking office he has increased combat forces in Afghanistan, expanded our air strikes in Pakistan, shifted the fighting in Iraq onto hired mercenaries and local soldiers, and pledged his "full support" to the "heroic" CIA. Obama doesn't want to end the war; he wants to fight it smarter, cutting our losses in some areas while stepping up attacks in others, aiming to salvage a partial victory. The new commander in chief has scaled down the grandiose goals that launched the war, replacing them with a fallback battle plan for maintaining some control over the Iraqi and Afghan governments, oil supplies, and pipeline routes.

So the war continues, now with less press coverage because when mercenaries and local soldiers die, it barely makes the news. The war continues because millions of Iraqis and Afghans refuse to accept US hegemony and are willing to die to defeat it. The war continues with no end in sight because Obama refuses to abandon this drive for hegemony.

He refuses not because he's evil but because too much is at stake. A defeat in this strategic area would be devastating. Many of the privileged leases that US petroleum companies own on Mideast oil would be canceled. These favorable leases help keep fuel and petrochemical prices comparatively low in the USA. Without them, prices would soar, eliminating much of our economic advantage. The loss of this competitive edge would mark the decline of American dominance. It would be particularly disastrous for the US military, which is the world's largest consumer of oil. We would become one player among several, no more powerful than the European Union, Russia, China, or India. Obama knows that any US president who moved in such an egalitarian direction would be out of office very soon.

The corporate elite backed him because he could calm the waters of discontent and create superficial changes that would allow them to maintain their power. His eloquence and charisma revived hope in America. We want so much to believe him that we overlook that he's still killing thousands of our fellow human beings. Obama is proving to be the ultimate cosmetic change. His performance is another American triumph of image over actuality.

A similar swindle occurred in the 2006 election campaign. The Democrats won control of the Senate and House of Representatives by promising to end the war. Instead, a few months later they voted a huge increase in military spending and supported US troop surges.

These betrayals of democracy make it clear our government doesn't really represent us but rather the business interests. If they need cheap oil, the president and Congress will make war to get it for them, with time-out every few years for some campaign rhetoric about peace.

As disappointment turns to despair, peace activists are seeking new ways to confront state power and stop this killing machine. We've moved beyond demonstrations and petitions into direct action, defying the government's laws and impeding its capacity to wage war. *Radical Peace: People Refusing War* portrays these efforts. Telling the first-person experiences of war resisters, deserters, and peace activists from the USA, Europe, Iraq, and Afghanistan, it's a journey along diverse paths of nonviolence, the true stories of people working for peace in unconventional ways.

The book is a group effort with contributions from many activists. What ties us together is the conviction that being peaceful doesn't mean obeying violent governments. Confronted with implacable militarism, we've turned to radical measures to stop it. Our experiences offer many answers to the question, "How can I help end war?" Not all of us agree with every approach described here, but we all agree the stories deserve to be told.

Our hope is that by going public we will reveal the varied culture of resistance now flourishing within the peace movement and draw more people to it. The movement needs to grow. Only when enough of us act together will we be able to stop war.

This violence must end, and we, the people, are the only ones who can do it. The brutal power-mongers who rule most countries are too ignorant for the weapons they wield, and we can't let them keep killing. Their juggernaut of aggression continues to roll, crushing multitudes of soft, breathing human beings, creating more counter-violence at every turn, lumbering toward annihilation. Now none of us in any country is safe.

Most of us involved with this book are criminals because we violate that travesty of American freedom, the Patriot Act. In order to survive in these times of infiltration and surveillance, we're not an organized group but a loose network with many cutouts between us. Rather than coordinated plans, we rely on spontaneous opportunities. The government will send us to prison if it can, and since none of us wants that, names have been changed to protect the guilty. I'm the real-name spokesperson because I live outside the "homeland." Plus as a former Special Forces sergeant I'm used to being under attack.

Each chapter tells a different story. Some are told in the voices of the actors. Every one is intensely personal, sometimes brutally so. But all delineate journeys heading somehow toward peace.

Come along with us.

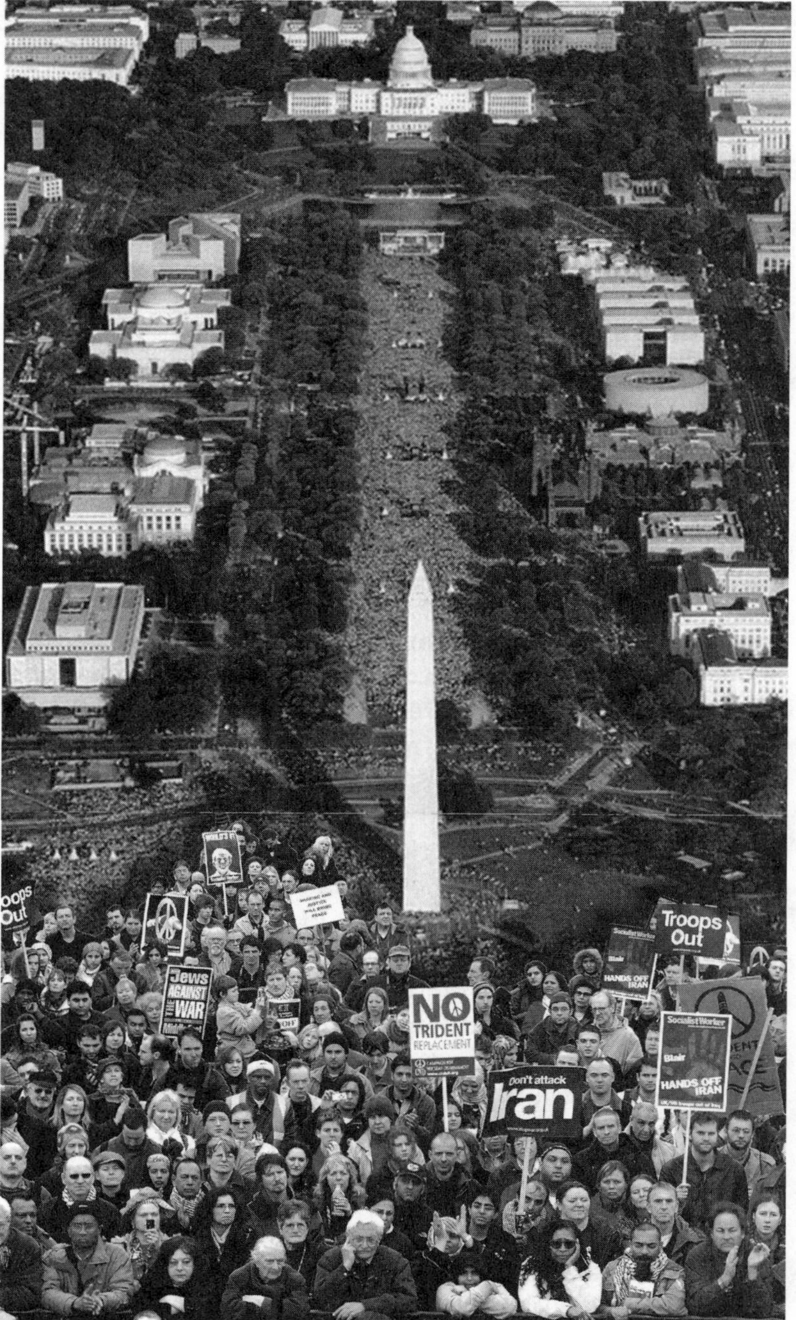

Troops Out
Troops Out
Jews AGAINST THE WAR
NO TRIDENT REPLACEMENT
Don't attack Iran
Socialist Worker
Blair
HANDS OFF IRAN
Socialist Worker
Blair
HANDS OFF IRAN

— 1 —

The Real War Heroes

"That must be them." Petra took one hand off the steering wheel and pointed to a group of soldiers about two hundred meters away, standing along our road next to a high chain link fence topped with barbed wire.

Traffic was light, but Petra said, "I don't want *any* other cars around." She pulled off the road and stopped. "Get everything ready."

I crawled into the back of the car and opened the rear hatch to give access to the interior and to raise the license plate out of sight. We wore caps and sunglasses to be less recognizable.

When the road was empty, she started driving again. We approached the soldiers, who were walking in the grass, stopping often to pick things off the ground and put them in sacks they were dragging.

"There's Rick." Petra slowed and drove along the shoulder. A man turned his head at the sound of our car crunching gravel, dropped his bag, and ran towards us with a slight limp. While the guards shouted for him to stop, I thrust my arm out, grabbed Rick's hand, and pulled. He lunged forward and dived into the open hatch, banging his leg on the edge. A guard was swearing and groping at the holster on his belt. Rick scrambled in, knocking off his glasses, and Petra floored the gas. Our spinning tires hurled gravel behind us then squealed over the pavement. The car slid halfway across the road before Petra brought it under control, and we sped away.

One guard was waving his pistol at us but not aiming it, and the other was punching buttons on a cell phone. Some of the detention soldiers were clapping and shouting envious congratulations, others just stood staring.

I closed the hatch as Petra rounded a corner and headed for the autobahn. Rick lay on the floor trembling and gasping, holding his leg in pain. I gripped him on the shoulder to steady him. "Way to go! You're on your way out of the Army."

His tension exploded into laughter, then tears. "Thanks, thanks," he spluttered.

"It's not over yet," Petra said.

Rick breathed deeply, scrinched his eyes to block the tears, and clenched his fists. "Not going back."

I tried to calm my own tremors.

Petra drove away from the base through a section of fast-food franchises and striptease bars that bordered it. Rick put his glasses back on; bent at the bow, they sat crookedly on his nose. We put up the rear seat so we could sit without attracting attention, then waited at the stoplight by the autobahn entrance for thirty seconds that seemed like ten minutes, surrounded by other cars full of American soldiers and German civilians, none of whom noticed us. Finally Petra roared up the onramp. German autobahns have no speed limits, and soon the Volkswagen was going flat out at 160 kilometers per hour.

From a small suitcase I pulled out civilian clothes for Rick, and he started stripping off his uniform. "Last time I'll ever wear this thing."

As he took off his shirt, I got a whiff of the sour stench of fear, which I knew well from my own time in the military. He stuffed the fatigues into a trash bag, then put on corduroy pants and a cotton sweater. Now he looked like a young German, but with the buzz cut hair, almost like a neo-Nazi. I set my cap on his head.

At the first rest stop we pulled in and parked beside a van. I gave him the suitcase and a wallet with a thousand euros in it. We shook hands, then hugged. I clapped him on the back. He got out of the car and kissed Petra on the cheek, crying again as he thanked us. With a combination of a glare and a grin, he pushed the bag with his uniform into a garbage can. I got into the front seat of the VW; Rick got into the back of the van, giving us a V sign. The van pulled away, headed for Sweden, where Rick would apply for asylum.

Petra re-entered the autobahn, much slower now because she too was crying, quietly, with a resolute face. "He's out of the war," she said in her throaty German accent. "No one's going to kill him, and he's not going to kill anybody." She took the next exit, then wended back over country roads towards her home. "Now I'm exhausted."

"Me too, all of a sudden," I said. "This one was hairy. We broke more laws than usual."

"Good. Such laws need to be broken. I'll make us some coffee."

Petra had been the first of our group to meet with Rick. She worked in Caritas, the German Catholic social agency, and a priest had brought him to her office. Rick was absent without leave, AWOL, from the Army, determined not to go back, but didn't know what to do. He'd heard from another soldier that the Catholic church sometimes helped, so he went there.

The priest was in too public a position to personally do much, but he introduced him to Petra because she was active in Pax Christi, the Catholic peace movement. The priest and the social worker had a tacit "don't ask, don't tell" agreement about her counseling work with soldiers. She didn't volunteer information, and he didn't pry.

Petra had various approaches to freeing soldiers. She could help them apply for conscientious objector status, but these days CO applications were usually turned down by the military. She had a degree in clinical psychology and was skilled at teaching GIs how to get psychological discharges, to act the right amount of crazy and handle the trick questions the military shrinks would throw at them.

But now those too were usually denied. The military needed bodies — didn't care if they were crazy bodies.

If neither of these methods worked, and if the soldiers were desperate to get out, she would help them desert, a drastic step because it risked years in prison for them and major hassles for her.

Petra has never been arrested, but based on experiences of others in our group, she could expect to be charged with accessory to military desertion and with aiding and abetting a fugitive. The court process would be a severe drain on the energy and finances of both her and our group, but it is unlikely that she'd actually go to prison. With public opinion already so opposed to this war, the German government wouldn't want to risk the protests. But she'd probably get a year on probation, lose her job, and have trouble finding another one.

Why did she take the risk? Petra's grandfather had been an SS trooper, the kind of Christian who unquestioningly supports authority. His children reacted by becoming atheists. Petra became the kind of Christian who opposed authority, including the church hierarchy. She felt stopping war was more important than her personal security.

When she met Rick, she was impressed by his sincerity and also his desperation. He told her he'd got married after high school to a co-worker at a restaurant, an illegal immigrant from El Salvador who was a few years older. They wanted to have children but couldn't raise them on minimum wage. He wanted to become an electrical engineer but couldn't afford college. The Army's offer of tuition aid and electronics training was better than life at Pizza Hut, so he enlisted in 2001.

The plan was that she'd work in the towns where he was stationed. After his four-year hitch, he'd go to college while she continued to work, and after college when he had a good job, they'd have kids. Eight years seemed like a long time to get started in life, but by then he'd have a real career.

After 9/11, the Army needed infantry troops more than electronic specialists, so they took away his needle-nosed pliers, gave him an M-16, and flew him to Afghanistan. First they made him excavate corpses, hoping to find bin Laden's, from the collapsed caves of Tora Bora, full of the reek of rotting meat. Then they sent him on night ambush missions along the Pakistan border: staring out from a machine gun bunker with goggles that made everything glow green and yellow, shooting anything that moved after dark, shipping the bodies out in the morning on the supply helicopter, still hoping to find bin Laden. Finally he was assigned to round up men from the villages around Kandahar and send them to interrogation camps. But there weren't many men in the villages. They were either dead or in the mountains, and the Army didn't have enough troops to comb the mountains.

After eight months his wife divorced him.

In one of the villages an old woman walked by them with her goat. The goat wore a pack basket. The woman reached down, patted the goat, and blew them all up.

Rick woke up lying in a helicopter surrounded by dead and wounded friends. He felt he'd become one of his ambush victims being shipped out. The Army would be disappointed to find out he wasn't bin Laden.

It turned out later the woman was the mother of two sons who had been killed by the Americans.

With shrapnel wounds, a fractured leg, and a twisted spine, Rick was evacuated to the US hospital in Landstuhl, Germany, where after five months of treatment he was pronounced fit for active duty and given orders for Iraq. By then he'd heard about Iraq from other patients. He panicked, went AWOL, then met Petra.

She helped him clarify his options. He could apply for conscientious objector status or a psychological discharge, but with orders into a combat zone, his chances of success were nil. But if he deserted, there was a good chance that Sweden would accept his application for asylum.

Rick told Petra later that what finally settled his decision to desert was learning that in Sweden the state helps pay college expenses. You don't have to join the military and kill people just to get an education.

But before our group could make arrangements, Rick got arrested for AWOL and assigned to the detention barracks.

If they'd known he was planning to desert, they would've locked him in the stockade, but simple AWOL has become too widespread for that. He was busted down two ranks and assigned to sixty days hard labor, at the end of which he'd be sent to Iraq still under detention.

After visiting him in the detention barracks, Petra told us he seemed like a man on death row. His psychological condition was deteriorating so rapidly that she was afraid he would kill himself rather than go back to war. He begged her to try to get him out.

The current work detail for the detention soldiers was twelve hours a day of picking up trash along the fence at the boundary of the base. They'd finished inside the base and had just started working on the outside, a group of ten detainees with two guards.

Petra and I wouldn't have risked the snatch inside the base, but we were pretty sure the guards wouldn't fire their pistols outside the base for fear of "collateral damage." Shooting the local population is bad for public relations.

I alerted our sanctuary network in Germany and Sweden and arranged the logistics to get Rick into a new life.

Since I'm a US citizen, if I got arrested for helping soldiers desert, I'd be sent back to the "homeland" for trial and probably to prison. It's worth the risk to me, though.

I do this work because my past is similar to Petra's grandfather's. I was in the Special Forces in Panama and Vietnam. I'd joined the Green Berets to write a book about war. During our search-and-destroy operations, I kept telling myself, "I'm just here gathering material for a novel." But our deeds have consequences that affect us and others regardless of why we do them. I'm still dealing with the repercussions from my involvement, and my work in the military resistance movement is a way of atoning for it.

I've met many veterans who never saw combat but still feel a burden of guilt. Just being part of an invading force and abusing another country pollutes the soul. Under the hyperbole, there's some truth in Kurt Tucholsky's statement, "All soldiers are murderers." The military exists to kill people, and everyone in it contributes to that. Even as civilians, we finance it.

Having got medals for combat, I know that the real heroes are the people like Rick who refuse to go, who stand up to the military and say no. If they're caught, the government punishes them viciously because they're such a threat to its power. Deserters and refusers are choosing peace at great danger to themselves. I wish I'd been that morally aware and that brave.

When this book is published, I'll have to stop actively participating in desertions and will have to break off direct contact with our group. Once I go public, my e-mails and phone calls will probably be routed through Langley, Virginia, and that would endanger our whole operation.

Ironically enough, when I left the Special Forces, the CIA offered me a job. If I had accepted it, I could now be another G-13 civil servant perusing the messages of dissidents, trying to find ways to neutralize us. The road not taken.

Now living in Germany, I can see how important it is to resist such things in their early stages. In the 1930s many Germans were afraid to oppose their government as it became increasingly vicious, hoping it wouldn't get too bad, hoping they'd be spared, hoping it would end soon, but then bitterly regretting their passivity after it was too late.

Better to go down resisting. Better yet to change it while we still can. It's clear now that Obama isn't really going to change things, so we have to do it ourselves.

— 2 —

Comrades in Arms

Hi Mr. Hathaway,

I got your letter (forwarded) asking for information for your book. To answer your first question, Yes, I'm enjoying living in Holland. I'm becoming the little Dutch girl — the little black Dutch girl, but that doesn't bother people here. They're very tolerant and internationally minded.

As for the rest of your questions, at first I didn't think I could answer them. They reminded me too much of an essay test in school. Plus it's not exactly pleasant to remember back on all this stuff, you know. I'm trying to leave it behind and start a new life.

But I kept thinking about it and finally decided I would forget the questions and just write about what happened. Like you said, people should know about this. Don't give anybody my address, though. The Army still wants to put me in prison.

Compared to a lot of people, I had it easy in Iraq — on a huge base with a Burger King, cold beer, video games, movies, air conditioned trailers, baseball games. About once a month we got mortared or rocketed and had to dive into the bunkers and maybe every other time somebody got killed, but there were thousands of us, so usually you didn't know them even though you felt bad for them.

Although it wasn't very dangerous, we had to work our tails off, shifts of twelve on, twelve off, seven days a week — you felt like a zombie. I was a data entry clerk, sitting in front of a computer typing stuff in. My eyes were fried, and I was on meds for migraines. When you weren't working, all you wanted to do was forget everything. When you were working, you wanted to forget it even more.

We had a big mental health clinic, and they sent combat troops there for evaluation and therapy. These guys were a wreck. I know because I had to type up some of the reports. The shrinks would try to get them on the right mix of tranks and anti-depressants, and they'd run therapy groups where the GIs would talk about what they'd been through, and then the docs would send them back, unless they thought they might kill themselves or another American, in which case they'd cycle them through again.

One of our cooks hung out with these guys, and he'd tell us their stories. Mostly it was about how much they hated the hajis[1] because you could never tell who was a terrorist and who wasn't. An IED would go off beside the road and kill your buddy, and you didn't know who set it. Maybe it was one of those people watching. You wanted to kill them all. A haji would fire some shots into your patrol, then disappear into the crowd. They were hiding him. You wanted to kill them all.

As the spoon was telling the stories, you could tell how mad he was about it. He had a safe job, but he really identified with the combat guys and what they were going through. He said the Arabs were cowards; they were afraid to stand up and fight fair, so they sneak around. They use car bombs and kidnap people for hostages. They're chicken-shit wimps. They know they'd lose a fair fight, he'd say, and his mouth would twist around.

I told him, What's so fair about the way we fight? Flying way up above someone where they can't shoot back and dropping a bomb on them. Blowing up a whole apartment building to get one sniper, who's probably already left. I said it seems to me taking a hostage is better than just killing somebody. It gives the other side a chance to save his life.

---

1 Originally an honorific title in Arabic for one who has made the hajj, the pilgrimage to Mecca, haji is used by US troops as a derisive term for an Iraqi.

He asked me whose side I was on and gave me a look like he wanted to shoot me. I said I was on the side of going home and giving these people their country back.

He got really pissed then, called me a haji whore, said I was probably blowing them all. He was shaking, he was so mad at me.

I just left. No point talking to somebody like that.

Couple of days later I had to go to the latrine in the middle of the night. The latrine was two sections of Porta-Potties between the women's and men's shower rooms and next to the mortar bunkers. It was all pretty ugly, but the flies loved it, so we had electric bug zappers mounted around the area — whenever you went out there you had to listen to the crackle and pop of bugs being fried.

The cook came out of one of the men's potties, zipping up. I looked the other way, hoping he wouldn't notice me, but he walked up to me. I figured he was going to call me another name. Or just maybe he might apologize for the ones he'd called me. Instead he looked around to make sure no one else was there, then grabbed me with one hand over my mouth, the other on my throat.

He shoved me into one of the women's potties, said he'd kill me if I screamed, and locked the door from the inside. He was squeezing my throat so hard I was afraid he was going to kill me anyway. He pushed me down and made me sit on the toilet. As soon as I did, I peed on myself, I was so scared. He unzipped and said, "You're going to give me some of what you've been giving the hajis." He pulled my hair real hard, yanked my head down, and stuck his thing in my mouth. Disgusting. I won't say what he said he'd do to me if I bit it.

He called me more names while he was squirting, then he twisted my hair, stuck his fist in my eye, and told me to swallow. I swallowed and he laughed. I won't say what he said he'd do to me if I told anyone.

After he left, I was shaking and couldn't get my breath. I've never felt worse in my life — helpless, worthless, little, like one of the bugs sizzling in the traps. I needed to throw up. I grabbed a plastic bag from the dispenser on the wall and got most of the puke into that. The bag was small, for used tampons, so a lot of it went over my hands. I knotted the bag and stuffed it into another bag.

I felt so filthy I wanted to die. The only thing that kept me going was rage. I knew if I killed myself, the guy would get away with this. To get back at him, I had to stay alive.

Crying all the while, I washed my hands, brushed my teeth for ten minutes, took a shower, washed my hair. Heart pounding, body twitching, I lay in my bunk trying to blank my mind until reveille finally played over the loudspeakers.

I wasn't hungry, and I knew if I went into the mess hall, he'd be there, asking me if I wanted my eggs scrambled or sunny-side up. I went to the office, and as soon as first sergeant came in from breakfast, I told him what the guy did and what he threatened to do to me if I told. The first sergeant told me to go see the medics and come back when I was done.

The medics asked me if I wanted an exam. I said no, I wanted them to examine what was in the bag for DNA evidence that the guy had raped me. They said they didn't have a forensic lab, but they could store the specimen in the refrigerator until the CID[2] told them what to do with it. They gave me a receipt marked "stomach contents."

When I went back to the first sergeant, he said I was being transferred to another base for my protection. I got mad. I said I didn't want to be transferred, I wanted to file a rape complaint and have the guy transferred to jail. He said that since the guy threatened me, the top priority had to be my safety. I said I'll be safe when he's in jail. The first sergeant said they can't put him in jail until after they investigate, and that'll take awhile, and in the meantime my protection is more important. The guy won't know where you are.

I said let me file the complaint first. He went to the file cabinet, took out a form, and handed it to me: Sexual Harassment Report. I told him this wasn't harassment, it

2 Now the Criminal Investigation Command, CID remains the acronym, stemming from its origin as the Criminal Investigation Division. It is the US Army's principal law enforcement agency responsible for the conduct of criminal investigations for all levels of the Army anywhere in the world.

was rape. He said this was the only form he had for that sort of thing. The CID could change it to rape later.

I didn't want to fill out that form. I went to the CID, but they wouldn't listen to me at all. They said all reports have to come through the chain of command — they don't accept what they called "wildcat reports."

By now it was clear I was getting the bureaucratic run-around. I was afraid if I got transferred out before the report got to the CID, it would never get there. So I went back and raised hell with the first sergeant. That helped. He could tell I wasn't lying and he knew the cook, so he said he'd make a deal with me. If I went ahead with the transfer today, he'd make sure the company commander forwarded the report to the brigade commander, and then he'd check with CID to make sure they got it.

I thought about it. I really didn't want to see that slimy spoon again. The thought of being totally away from him was very appealing. I needed a change. So I filled out the form, said a few good-byes, packed my duffel bag, and rode the convoy to the next base.

It was only about ten miles away, but this was one of the few times I'd really seen Iraq since I came in country. The place was a wreck — blown up houses, boarded up stores with bullet holes in the walls, twisted metal that used to be cars, men looking at you with hate in their eyes, women looking away. I wondered if any of the women had been raped by GIs or their own men. I would've liked to have talked to them, but they'd probably hate me for what I'm a part of.

The bay of the truck I was riding in had sandbags on the floor to protect from mines. A Blackwater shooter stood behind a machine gun mounted on the cab. I held my rifle pointed out but didn't think I could shoot anybody. I remembered back to when I'd joined the Army for college tuition help. I thought about what had happened to me and what my country was doing to the people here. I just cried.

My new company was pretty much like my old one, and my job was the same. After two weeks I got a report saying the specimen had been examined and no sperm was found, so the complaint was dismissed due to lack of evidence.

I wrote a letter to CID asking how many samples had been taken in the specimen and got a reply back saying they didn't comment on criminal investigations. I went to the Judge Advocate trying to get a lawyer to file an appeal and order a new lab test, but they said there weren't legal grounds for an appeal.

It filled me with fury that the guy was going to get away with this ... and probably do it again. I went to my new first sergeant and raised hell. This time it didn't help. He said all the procedures had been followed and I had to accept the result. If I didn't stop making trouble, he would have the company commander flag my personnel file so I wouldn't get promoted.

I fell apart, crying and shaking like after the rape. I didn't care about getting promoted, I told him, but I did care that I was being raped by the Army bureaucracy. He called the company clerk and told her to take me to Mental Health.

They gave me tranks and put me in a woman's therapy group. The group was quite an experience. It was run by a psychiatric nurse and had about twenty members, all of them had been abused by men they worked with. My story was actually one of the milder ones. I hadn't been pounded with fists or tied up and raped by three guys. I hadn't been burned with cigarettes or scarred on the face with a bayonet. But what happened to me was worse than some of the other cases — the woman who'd been mentally pressured into sex by her sergeant major and the one who'd had her hair cut off by her jealous boyfriend. All in all, we were quite a crew — the walking wounded. And most of the guys had got away with it.

During single therapy with the nurse I pleaded with her to help me get out of the Army. She said she had been able to get some people discharged, but only when their work record was terrible and their attitude was affecting others, in other words, when the Army knew it would be better off without them. It would take many very unpleasant months for me to build that kind of record, she said. In the meantime the Army would punish me in all sorts of ways for screwing up, and she didn't think I could take that kind of pressure. But she might be able to get me transferred out of country for mental health reasons. To do that, though, she'd have to write a report that made me seem like a total basket case, and that would mean no promotions or privileges.

No problem with that, I said, as long as I get out of here. I started crying then, and to my surprise she started crying too.

She told me that seeing what was going on here had totally turned her against the military. She said that abuse here is worse than stateside because the soldiers are part of a machinery of destruction, and that brings out the worst in people. Especially since we know deep down that this is an immoral war, our own morals tend to get lost too.

She wanted to just quit, but she had only sixteen months left until early retirement, and she needed to stick it out. In the meantime she was glad to help others get out.

Two weeks later I was in Germany and incredibly relieved. The atmosphere was very different. There wasn't this ghoulish backdrop of violence to everything, and I felt safe from both terrorists and rapists.

But I couldn't fit in. I just wasn't a soldier anymore. Everything we were doing seemed totally stupid, and I couldn't ignore that it was all helping the military do its basic job — killing people. I couldn't kowtow to these lames anymore, salute and say Sir and Ma'am. I sort of did it, but they could tell I didn't mean it, that I was dissing them. I started getting into trouble. I got an Article 15 for talking back to a captain and got restricted to barracks for coming back late from a weekend pass.[3] I got demoted to Pfc for insubordination — I had refused to shine my shoes and polish my brass for a brigade inspection, and our platoon got gigged[4] because of it. I still had twenty months to go on my enlistment, and I knew I had to get out now or I'd end up spending the rest of that time in jail. I didn't want to give

3 Article 15 of the Uniform Code of Military Justice, which permits commanders to discipline subordinates for lesser offences nonjudicially, i.e., without a court-martial.

4 An official reprimand for a minor delinquency and/or the punishment meted out.

the Army any more of my life but didn't have any idea how to escape.

I remembered hearing about an underground group that helps people get out, but I didn't know how to get in touch with them. I remembered seeing a peace sign and a PACE banner in a window in Ramstein, so I went there on my next pass.

It turned out to be a little radical office, two friendly, scruffy people sitting on scruffy furniture with anti-war posters on the wall and lots of books. They were German pacifists, but they told me they couldn't help me desert because they'd get arrested. They'd already been busted once for helping someone who turned out to be an agent. They said their phones and e-mail were tapped; they weren't sure if by the Germans or Americans. There was a good chance their office was bugged, so they couldn't even talk about doing anything illegal. About all they could do was picket and put up posters.

I told them what it was like in Iraq and what had happened to me and how it was with me now. They looked at me carefully and listened carefully, like the nurse had. When I finished, one of them stood up and motioned me to come outside. Out on the street, she scribbled something on a piece of paper and gave it to me, told me I should call this number, but only from a public phone and not on the base. She squeezed my hand and kissed me on the cheek.

It turned out to be your phone number, Mr. Hathaway. You know what happened after that, but I'll say it anyway because you asked me to. Then I'll bring you up to date on what I've been doing since we last saw each other.

First I met with you and some other people. I had to tell my story again and answer lots of questions. I had to bring copies of my rape report and my disciplinary write-ups. I guess the group was trying to see if I was an agent. At first I thought that was dumb — if I was an agent, I could fake those. But then I thought maybe if they're faked and the group gets arrested, you could get the case thrown out for entrapment.

I was very relieved when the group decided I was for real. I could tell you all really cared about me.

My actual desertion was so simple. You gave me a train ticket to Holland and the way to contact the safe house. You gave me money (that was very nice!) and a big good-bye hug (also nice!).

I was scared on the train. I felt totally alone and at the same time afraid everyone could tell just by looking at me that I was deserting. I was riding off into a whole new life and had no idea what it would be — happiness, prison, poverty, another rape?

The people in the safe house were wonderful. They took me right in and made me feel at home. They were risking jail to help me, and the group in Germany had been too, and I'm really grateful to you all for the good new life I have now.

First I got new clothes, a place to live, then a job — data entry again, but better pay, shorter hours, and a lot nicer people. I still have this background worry that the Army will catch me and lock me up, but at this point it's not very likely. If they knew which town I was living in, they could probably track me down, but the Army doesn't have enough soldiers to really search for all the deserters. They need the ones they've still got for Iraq and Afghanistan. As long as I don't get into trouble here (I'm very careful!), I'm probably safe until my passport expires. That's in eight years, and by then I can apply for Dutch citizenship. As soon as I'm good at the language (it's hard!), I can go to college here (it's almost free!).

I miss my family a lot, though. My sister got married last month, and it really hurt that I couldn't go back for the wedding. The MPs would probably be waiting to greet me at the airport. I'm hoping my family will visit me here — I think they'd like it. They might not like some of the changes I've gone through here, though.

I became friends with one of the women who works at the safe house. Then we became more than friends. This happened gradually. I'd never gone in that direction before, and it took some adjusting to.

Some of this change was because I got to thinking about how armies and war really are a man thing. They let women in because they need the bodies, but we really don't belong there. It hurts us to be part of such a thing. We try to cover up and forget the hurt, to prove we can take it, we're good enough for the man's world.

But now I see it's really the opposite — the man's world isn't good enough for us. But they have the power. They say how things are going to be, and we have to fit into that.

Even the way people have to work — rush to a job in the morning, work all day, come home at night exhausted and brain-dead, all just to get enough money to live on. I'm sure that must've been invented by a man — the owner of the factory where the rest of us have to work. Working all day long is no way to live, especially if you have a family, children who need to be taken care of. But a woman either has to do that or give up her power to a man who does it. The whole thing fits together — wars, factories, families all run by men.

And look where it's got us. We're killing each other, we're killing Mother Earth, everybody's miserable, nobody's happy, but men are afraid to change. They're terrified of losing their control. Power is everything to them — if it's gone, they're nothing, little boys again.

The whole thing has made me kind of sick of men (please don't take that personally — one of the reasons I like your novels so much is that they show you're trying to change all this too). I really needed to get away from the male world. So I'm trying something different.

And being with a woman is definitely different, we're more tuned in to one another. I've discovered that men aren't necessary to be happy in this world. Women are quite special, and I'm glad to be Nynke's lover.

I was raised to believe this was unnatural, but now that seems ridiculous. The whole idea that some things people do are natural and other things unnatural doesn't really make sense — people are part of nature, and other animals sometimes do it that way. To say it's unnatural is just a way of saying, "I don't like it," but hiding behind some big authority like God or Mother Nature.

Going through this change made me see that other things we believe are also probably nonsense. Most people believe that war is natural — we've always had wars, humans are just warriors, that's the way it has to be. They say the important thing is that we win. We need a strong military or another country will take us over. People are born violent, and we have to defend ourselves against that.

But this may be just the way things are now. In the future things might not have to be this way. It could be that this argument that human nature is violent is being put out by people who want to keep us from changing.

Our ancestors believed all sorts of bullshit was natural, made that way by God — kings had the right to rule over us, blacks were inferior to whites, women should obey men. When some people started to change those, conservatives screamed just like today that we can't change them, don't even try. But they were wrong.

I admit that doesn't mean they'd always be wrong. Some things might be built into humans, and maybe we can't do anything about them. It's hard to know for sure what those things are, but here's a way to find out. Let's start changing things. Let's change our ideas of how women and men are supposed to be. Let's change what it means to work. Let's outlaw nuclear weapons, then all military weapons. Let's make war illegal. How do we know it won't work until we've tried it?

Then after a long time of trying, at least a hundred years, what we haven't been able to change, that might be hardwired into us. We might have to just accept that. But we won't know until we've really tried. No harm in trying. I think we'll be surprised how much we can change.

Sincerely,
Larissa

— 3 —

Comparing Evils

Jamal Khan is an Afghan journalist who fled his country because of Taliban persecution and now lives in Germany. We met in the apartment of a mutual friend from the *Deutsche Friedensgesellschaft,* the German Peace Society. Jamal is mid-forties, thin, with curly brown hair, tan skin, and clear green eyes that take everything in. Though Jamal has some English ability, we spoke in German, and later reworked the interview together from my English translation.

Hathaway*: "Do you miss your country?"*
Khan: "Only when I'm drunk, which isn't very often. Then I get stupidly sentimental.

"Actually I'm not a big fan of any country. They're all inhuman. They exist mainly as platforms for power. The rulers promote cultural rituals that make people identify with the place they live. Then they manipulate the people's patriotic emotions to get them to fight wars for them. We cling to the identification because it gives us a sense of security, of belonging to something greater. But the insecurity we feel is actually generated by the power the rulers have over us.

"Nationalism is really a mental illness. Breaking the hold these national identities have on us would be an enormous improvement for the world.

"Afghanistan has the same patriotic crap, the fatherland, hierarchies of male power. So I don't miss it. But every day I miss my family and friends there."

"What did the Taliban do to you that made you leave?"
"Threatened to kill me. That was enough."

"Was that because you're gay?"
"No." Jamal lit a cigarette and gave me an irritated look. "Not everything about a person revolves around their sexuality, you know. The Taliban didn't know I was gay. I was discreet about that. They threatened to kill me because I'm a journalist and I ridiculed them in my articles. They actually did kill the newspaper editor. After that I left.

"But yes, it's much easier to be gay in Europe than in Afghanistan, and that's another reason I'm glad to be here."

"How did you get out?"
"The German embassy. They had a refugee program, and I filed a petition there. Then I bought an airline ticket, said tearful good-byes, and flew away. It wasn't such a police state that you couldn't get out. The difficult thing was to be accepted by another country. And back then the Germans were very good about that."

"Not now?"
"Less so."

"How do you feel about the Taliban compared to the current government?"
"That's difficult to answer. Both governments are terrible but in different ways. The Taliban were — still are — brutal fanatics. And yes, they did kill gays. They caught two guys making love, dragged them through the streets, and stoned them to death. Really horrible. They're hysterical homophobes; it totally freaks them out. The whole society is very repressed about this. If you're queer, you have to stay in the closet, even now. But if you did stay there, the Taliban didn't break into the closet and kill you. They didn't want to know about it.

"Women were persecuted too. If they were openly Western, they could get into major trouble, even be killed.

"All that's despicable, and I'm glad there's less of it now.

"But there's another side to this. Western propaganda uses this to whip up war fever. The media in Europe and North America have seared all sorts of atrocity stories — some of them true, some of them not — into people's minds to justify invading the country and bombing the people.

"The Taliban are bad guys, no doubt about it. I'm not fond of them at all. They killed hundreds of people, including friends of mine. They would've killed me if I had stayed.

"But the USA has killed fifty thousand Afghans just in this current war ... and more every day. They're devastating the country. They make the Taliban look like boy scouts."

"How do you like it here in Germany?"
"I'm glad to be here. I'm glad they let me in. I'm not so glad they're trying to throw me out now."

"How's that? What's happened?"
"I had refugee status as long as the Taliban were in power because they were the ones who threatened me. But when the USA installed this new government, the Germans said I had to go back because now I wouldn't be killed. I can understand their position. But it would drive me crazy to see what the USA is doing there, to live in the middle of that. I'd probably join the Taliban!" Jamal gave a tormented laugh and dragged on his cigarette.

"So I went underground. I'm illegal here now. That means I can't hold a regular job. I have to worry every time I see a cop, hoping he doesn't ask for my papers. I work as a cook now where they pay me cash, no benefits, no health insurance. I publish articles here and there, but I can't be employed anywhere. It's a pain, a real struggle just to live.

"Sometimes the police raid the places where illegals work. They round them up and send them back to whatever country they came from. Last month they raided the restaurant where I worked. They did it before the customers arrived, so as not to upset them.

"Three cops barged from the dining room into the kitchen as we were working prep, shouted to everybody not to move and to show our papers. Three of us ran for the back door, but other police were blocking it. By now they knew we were the ones they wanted, so they closed in from both sides.

"One of us — an Iraqi woman — started crying hysterically. While the cops were trying to calm her down, I saw a chance.

"The wall into the dining room has an opening where we set the finished plates for the waiters to pick up. I dived at the opening, hurt my hip like hell going over it, and landed on the floor of the dining room. Police were shouting at me from the kitchen.

"By the time I got up, a cop who was guarding the front door was running towards me. I knocked over a table to block his way. The cop darted around it to cut me off. He was right behind me going out the door, but I was faster. It meant a lot more to me than it did to him. Plus he had a beer belly.

"I sprinted across the street, almost got hit by cars both ways. When I looked back, he was waiting for a break in the traffic. I didn't slow down. Sometimes they have a motorcycle backup, but I was lucky.

"I went back a couple of days later to get my pay, but the manager wouldn't give it to me, said I broke a bunch of dishes when I pushed over the table. The money he owed me was a lot more than the dishes, but what could I do, call the cops? He gave me back my coat, though.

"So I got another job. Lots of places want to hire us because we work so cheap. We're captive labor.

"I've worked picking strawberries and apples. Dug asparagus. Swept out movie theaters after the last show. Swamped out bars. Washed windows. I lugged around dead pigs in a slaughterhouse — at least that's better than eating them.

"I'd write a book too, if I didn't have to work all the time." Jamal gave me a look of envy with a bit of accusation in it.

"So my feelings about Germany are mixed. They saved my life by giving me asylum, but they're helping to kill thousands of my people. They know their own people are against this war, so they claim to be only a peace-keeping force, but they're really fighting on the side of the Americans. They have a whole squadron of spy planes that take pictures to show the Americans where to bomb. They've been teaching Afghan police and soldiers counter-insurgency tactics, but since that hasn't worked, now they've sent attack troops to kill the Taliban themselves. They're working with the USA to dominate the country and keep the puppet government in power.

"It's no wonder that the fanatics are trying to take vengeance here in Germany. They have to. Their friends are being murdered. Retribution is a matter of honor for them. That goes very deep."

"What do you think the Germans should do?"
"Stop supporting the American invasion. Pull out their troops and spy planes and go home."

"What should the USA do?"
"That's complicated. First we have to look at what they've done in the past. Throughout the seventies and eighties they did everything they could to overthrow the Afghan government. That government was Communist, and to the USA that meant it had to go, no matter how many people had to die.

"The people most willing to die killing Communists were the fanatical Muslims, who hated this secular government. The CIA helped them to attack it, starting with raids on outposts and assassinations of local officials. The government asked the Soviet Union for help, and they sent in troops. Then the CIA stepped up its involvement, recruiting thousands of *mujahideen*, training them, financing them, turning them into an army to attack the Soviets. It escalated into a full-scale war for ten years. Left two million dead, a lot of those children who starved in all the chaos. Brutalized the whole country. All the young people growing up knew was war. Savagery became their norm.

"The people the USA is now trying to kill — the Taliban, Osama bin Laden and al-Qaeda — they were all on its payroll then fighting the Communists. It was your government that turned them into killers. After they won the war, it was inevitable they'd take over the country. By then they were the strongest force.

"Once the Taliban was in power, the USA wasn't concerned that they were persecuting women and gays and non-Muslims. The Taliban were just one of the many dictatorships the USA does business with and doesn't object to.

"But that changed when the Taliban became anti-capitalist, as they shifted away from a corporate-dominated economy and towards Islamic socialism. That made them a danger to Western interests. The final straw was when they refused to allow a US company to build an oil pipeline through the country. Suddenly the Western press was full of stories about how evil the Taliban were. They became these monsters who needed to be destroyed before they took over the world.

"So the USA invaded, chased the Taliban back into the mountains, and put in their figurehead as president. This Hamid Karzai, he used to work for the US company that wants to build the pipeline. He's their guy! And the pipeline is at the top of his agenda ... if the war ever stops.

"Western media call this 'stability' and 'nation building,' but those are just PR slogans for a new kind of imperialism. For decades the USA has manipulated Afghanistan for its own economic and political purposes. So to finally answer your question, what it should do now is stop what it's been doing. It should demilitarize the country as much as possible, take back all the weapons it can, and just leave. Then it should use its power to convince other countries not to send in more arms.

"Yes, there'll be a war. But without foreign intervention it won't last so long.

"And yes, the Taliban will probably take over again. We'll have to learn to live with that for a while. The Taliban won't last forever. We'll gradually undermine their power, and they'll fall."

"But if everyone else gives up their weapons and the Taliban are the only ones who have them, they could rule for a long time."

"Could be. But peace with the Taliban would be better than war with the Americans. If other countries stay out of it, we can handle the Taliban. Nonviolently.

"There's no point in trying to overthrow governments with violence. It just poisons the culture. I've seen that first hand. Better to overthrow them with peace, render then irrelevant. In the long run, peace is stronger. If we always react peacefully, that will dissolve the violence ... eventually.

"At first things might get worse, because the violence we've done to others in the past is coming back on us. But if we stay peaceful, do as my cousin Jesus said and turn the other cheek, don't fall back into fear and brutality, we can ride out this phase of rebound violence and not make any more enemies. This is the only way I see to defuse the situation and break the cycle. As my neighbor Gandhi said, 'There is no way to peace, peace *is* the way.'[5]

"But I know most people don't agree with that. So many men still want to be macho warriors, want to fight. But I see that as a sign that they really feel very weak and afraid, so they have to go to the opposite extreme. That's why queers like me are so threatening to them. We show on the outside what they have on the inside. And they can't bear to face that. But they dream about it."

"So basically the USA should leave."
"Of course."

"Do you think that'll happen?"
"Of course not."

"Why not?"
"Because the corporations running the USA need that pipeline. It's not just something they'd like to have. They need it. The only way they can keep their present level of profits and hold on to their economic advantage is if they keep cheap oil flowing in. And that means controlling the pipeline.

5 Widely attributed to Gandhi, this quote originated with A.J. Muste, American peace activist and social reformer (1885-1967). Gandhi's statement is almost identical.

"These wars aren't about whether the USA will get the oil it needs. With a world market, no one can stop the USA from buying oil. The wars are about how much they're going to have to pay for it and how much they can control it. Dominating oil will give them economic leverage over other countries, and that's what they're after.

"They don't care how many people they kill to do that. They're not people themselves. They're corporations. They have to maximize their profits. That's the basis of their existence."

"What do you see in the future?"

"In forty-five minutes I go to the restaurant and start making salads. That's all." Jamal stood up and pulled some folded paper out of his jacket. "I brought along something I wrote. If you want, you can put it in your book. It's sort of a fable. About the damage being done to the most important resource in my country."

He handed me the pages:

Malalai

The laughter of young Malalai delighted the villagers whenever they heard it, which was often. They listened with silent smiles, for to have laughed in response would have broken the charm.

Laughter streamed from the girl in floating spheres of sound that reconnected everyone who heard it to an inner happiness they'd forgotten. The villagers never knew when she might laugh, but they'd learned that two things never caused it: someone's misfortune or an attempt to make her laugh. They had to wait and be surprised.

Malalai was often in the village, running errands for her mother, playing with friends, following the flight of a moth. She liked to stop by the spice shop with its big glass jars full of roots, leaves, seeds and powders. Although she was barely tall enough to reach them, she could unscrew the lids and peer inside, absorbing the colors and scents. Black salt smelled like matches and looked like dirt. Hing[6] was yellow as a bee and reeked like rotten radishes. Cloves were little black buds with the fragrance of carnations. Curry leaves smelled like her father on a hot day. Breathing cinnamon with her eyes closed was a happy dream; nutmeg, a dark, scary one. Coriander woke her up. Chilies made her sneeze. Ginger made her jump.

And all together they made her laugh. And when she did, the shop lady remembered again why she loved spices.

Malalai enjoyed the fabric store with its bolts of cloth: gossamer organdy, modest muslin, coarse burlap, sturdy canvas, busy paisley, comforting flannel, regal cashmere, filigreed lace. Aswirl with the profusion of textures and colors, she would laugh, and the man in store was again glad to be selling cloth.

Malalai spent lots of time in her father's business, watching as he turned wood into furniture and cabinets. She liked seeing him saw and plane and hammer and polish. She liked the scents of wood shavings, sawdust, linseed oil and varnish, and the stacks of slabs, planks and dowels. She learned the difference between oak for the few wealthy customers and pine for the many poor customers. She hated the shriek of the circular saw but loved how the chips flew. She was fascinated by the twisting drill bit that looked like it was climbing into the air but just went around and 'round.

Fine emery paper felt like her father's cheek if he hadn't shaved. Coarse sandpaper felt like stuck sugar but tasted terrible. Glue looked like honey but tasted even worse than sandpaper.

When her father finished a table or chair, he would set Malalai on it and ask her to dance to see if it wobbled. If it stood stable under her prancings and pirouettes, she would laugh and tell him, "Good work!"

---

6 Asafoetida, a plant native to South Asia, and widely used there as a food and digestive aid. Also known as stinking gum, it has a foul smell when raw, but provides a smooth flavor reminiscent of leeks in cooked dishes.

And her father would think, I'm a lucky man.

At home Malalai liked to help her mother cook. Sometimes this helping ended up causing more work for her mother, but the mother was happy to see her learning. She taught Malalai how to make fresh cheese, bringing milk to a foaming boil and drizzling in lemon juice. As soon as the acid hit, the milk would separate into watery whey and clumps of curd, and Malalai would laugh.

Her mother would smile and think, Now she's understanding transformation.

Their country had been invaded by soldiers from faraway, the USUKs. One day the foreigners drove into their village in big trucks. The USUKs were strange people. You couldn't tell what they really looked like because they wore thick clothes that made them seem swollen, hard hats that hid their hair, and goggles that hid their eyes.

The first time Malalai saw them she thought they had dressed up to look silly, so she laughed. Her father quickly hushed her and told her she must never laugh at these people.

One of the USUKs pointed at them and shouted in a strange language. The soldiers walked towards them with their rifles ready. They made her father and mother turn around and prop themselves against a wall with their hands. Malalai watched as the USUKs ran their hands all over her mother's and father's bodies, poking and feeling. Her mother was shuddering and crying. Her father held his mouth tightly shut. The soldiers smiled at Malalai. They talked among themselves while keeping their rifles aimed.

Then the USUKs let them go. As the family walked home, her father couldn't look at Malalai or her mother. His hands were trembling.

Malalai never laughed again.

— 4 —

Exit Free

The following report was sent by Naomi Golner, one of the founders of Exit Free, a collective that helps women leave the military by discharge or desertion.

I've become a criminal for peace. How I got here is a complicated story, beginning when the community college where I teach reduced most of its humanities faculty to adjunct status. It saved them a bundle on salaries. We now teach a maximum of three courses per semester, for a really miserable hourly wage with no benefits. They brought in other part-timers to fill the gaps. So the faculty are now mostly freelancers. I ended up with a lot less money but a lot more time.

Several other women I knew were also broke — laid off or dropped out of the McJob economy. We decided to share the misery and formed a collective to make ends meet. One of us had a big empty-nester house from her divorce settlement, so we all moved in. We buy food in bulk, share two cars, tend a big garden, help each other with the things each of us is good at, sometimes quarrel and cry, but mostly we like being together. We feel stronger now than before when it was each of us alone against the neo-con world.

We decided to do something useful with all our free time: make trouble. There's a military base nearby, and several of us knew soldiers there. The stories they told us about how they were treated made us mad. The things they were being sent overseas to do made us even madder. A lot of them told us they wanted very much to get out of the military, so we decided to help.

We chose the name Exit Free because it applies to our military work and also to our escaping from our own job prisons as much as possible. Exit Free has been around for three years now. We've got four women out of the war as COs, one as a refuser (but she's still in prison), and nine as deserters. None of the deserters has been caught. We're trying to get more staff so we can open it up to men.

The program starts with encouraging the soldiers to tell what they've been through, to get it off their chests. A lot of women who have served in Iraq and Afghanistan are traumatized by their experiences there. The brutality they were a part of is a continuing pain on their hearts. Some of them are filled with self-loathing even if they didn't personally do anything horrible. They know they were part of a death factory. And they know how much they were hated by the people there. Plus a lot of them were abused by the male GIs. Those guys do things over there they'd never do at home. It's like they got a license to act out their monster fantasies.

Our psychologist runs a therapy group for these women that helps them come to terms with what they've gone through. It's not that they leave it behind. This stuff goes too deep for that. But they can understand the whole thing better, get some perspective, some psychological distance from it.

A lot of other women are terrified of being sent over there. They've heard the stories, they've seen comrades come back wounded mentally and physically. They don't want to hurt other people, and they don't want to be hurt themselves.

Exit Free's program begins with our psychologist helping them understand why they joined in the first place. There are the surface reasons, like job training or getting away from a bad situation at home. But usually there are also deeper psychological motives, and the women need to confront those before they can really be free of it.

As they dig into this stuff, most of them discover that by joining the military they were unconsciously trying to become what their father wanted them to be: a son rather than a daughter. Becoming a soldier is usually one of a long series of attempts to win the old man's acceptance. Some of them have been so busy doing that for years that they don't know who they really are. Their selves have got lost in trying to conform to another person's expectations. Wending their way out of this and recovering their real identity is very difficult.

Rejecting the military can be the first assertion of their authentic personality. It's therapeutic — but painful.

Our patriarchal culture has really mangled us all. But once we've taken a stand against patriarchy and are willing to pay the price of opposing it, in other words, once we've given up on pleasing daddy and put that part of us to rest, then we come into a new sense of personal power. All sorts of possibilities open for us. We can become an Amazon warrior ... an earth mother ... a philosopher ... an artist. We can encompass all of that. But it starts by breaking free, and that's what we're helping the soldiers to do. And ourselves too.

Most of the women have learned firsthand the futility of violence. They've seen how it just produces more violence, more broken bodies, broken families, more hatred and revenge. They don't want anything to do with war. Since they've become true conscientious objectors, they have a legal right to be discharged as that, but the military makes it very difficult.

CO applications for religious reasons have the best chance. Fortunately the local Episcopal priest is a pacifist. She works with soldiers to deepen their spiritual understanding of nonviolence, helps them prepare their applications, writes attesting documents for them, and role-plays interviews with them with the sort of questions the board will ask.

Most of the applications still get rejected, but Jane has got several soldiers free, and that has caused her problems at church. It turns out that the commanding general of the base is a member of the parish. He doesn't attend regularly and wasn't aware that the priest does outreach ministry at Exit Free, but when it finally came to his attention, he got quite upset. First he tried to persuade her to stop, saying she should stick to religion and "render unto Caesar what is Caesar's." He explained that what she was doing was unpatriotic; it was damaging the effectiveness of our fighting forces, and surely she didn't want to do that.

Jane resisted her impulse to tell him that was exactly what she wanted to do, and instead talked about the sincerity of the applicants and how they really did meet the requirements for a CO discharge. She tried to persuade him to get the board to lighten up on its requirements. She invited him to meet with the soldiers and hear their stories firsthand. He declined and left.

Afterwards she told us that underneath his condescending paternalism he was clearly a very dangerous man.

The next round got uglier. Suddenly many of the military families canceled their pledges of financial support for the church. Not all, though. A few actually increased their pledges but asked that it be kept quiet.

An article appeared in the local paper about the priest's anti-military activities, and Jane started getting hate calls. Conservative civilians in the parish canceled their pledges, then took out an ad in the paper with the headline, "We support our troops, not our priest."

It totally polarized the congregation, and the financial effects were disastrous. Church income fell by a third. Attendance dropped. People accused Jane of destroying the church.

A delegation of "concerned Christians" tried to convince the bishop to fire her or transfer her to a church with no military facilities nearby — "in the interests of fairness." This priest was clearly prejudiced against the military, and the church shouldn't support prejudice.

Fortunately the bishop is a brave man. He refused and said if they were dissatisfied with Jane, they'd have to convince the vestry, a governing board of lay people elected by the congregation, to cancel her contract.

With that began the battle of the vestry. Serving on a vestry is one of those volunteer activities that appeal only to committed church members — lots of work for no pay. The vestry has to work closely with the priest, so the only people who want the job tend to be those who like the priest. Of the four vestry members, only one wanted her replaced. Another didn't approve of her CO activities but felt she had a right to do them. Two shared her pacifist sentiments. (Take a guess what the gender distribution was on this issue. You got it, two and two, men and women.)

Vestry elections were a few months away. The anti-Jane members of the congregation recruited a slate of candidates to "save the church." The pro-Jane members supported the incumbents and other candidates who wanted to keep their priest. The congregation seemed to be about equally divided, so both groups became seized with evangelical fervor and began recruiting new members. Many people associated with Exit Free attended the church already (Jane has a spiritual presence about her that inspires people), but now almost all of us found the Lord and showed up in the pews, some in military uniform. I joined myself — even though I'm really Jewish.

We won the election hands down. Seeing that there were actually more of us than of them was one of the great moments of my life. It filled me with hope. We can change this country.

Since then the general hasn't been to church.

Soldiers whose CO applications get turned down have three options, all of them terrible. They can try to get a psycho discharge, but it's very hard to act convincingly crazy when they've never felt more sane in their lives, the old Catch-22. Plus the military can lock them in its own mental hospitals and fill them full of drugs, so if they weren't crazy beforehand, they will be afterwards.

They can refuse to obey orders. If so, they'll be jailed for months, court-martialed, then sent to military prison for a year or so, and at the end of the sentence they're given a less-than-honorable discharge.

For people with great inner strength, that can be the right path. They are taking a clear moral stand. But the price they have to pay for that can be crushing. Prisons are terrible places that destroy human beings. It's very easy to get in trouble there and get your sentence extended. Some people never get out. Others emerge broken and embittered.

They can desert. If they're caught, they'll usually get a longer prison sentence than a refuser would. They can reduce the risk of arrest if they leave the country and don't return for many years. At some point after a war, Congress usually passes an amnesty allowing deserters to return. But that can be a long wait, separated from their family and cultural roots. It's also difficult to find a country that will grant asylum to a deserter. Traditionally Canada and Sweden have sheltered US deserters, but lately Canada has become less willing to displease Washington. They sometimes send people back to be arrested. Sweden is a long ways away, a strange language, a difficult climate.

Fortunately a new possibility has opened up. We've been able to get several Spanish-speaking deserters into Venezuela. The government there isn't afraid to defy Washington. They're showing great courage in standing up to a massive, multi-level attack by the USA and the old Venezuelan elite who want their power back.

One woman's story, Deeana's, is particularly interesting. She was born in New Jersey, but her family was originally from Puerto Rico. She came to us wanting help with a sexual harassment issue. Her sergeant was hitting on her. When she turned him down, he was convinced that just meant she wanted to be conquered, so he stepped up the pressure to show her his manly strength. He would brush up against her in the hall or touch her at her desk, but he was always careful that no one else could see.

Deeana eventually broke down and told him he was repulsive and disgusting, but rather than chasing him away, that turned him into an enemy. A powerful enemy. He started giving her all the worst work details and inventing reasons to write up disciplinary reports on her. But he made it clear that if she gave in, he would "treat her good." He was really enjoying the whole thing — a sadist. Plus it made his pathetic life less boring.

When she still wouldn't put out, he accused her of having an affair with a woman sergeant in the same company who was pretty clearly lesbian. Deeana didn't even bother to deny it, just walked away.

Then something weird happened. The woman sergeant actually did start hitting on her. She said she knew what the guy was up to and since she was a rank higher than he, she could protect Deeana from him ... if Deeana was nice to her.

Deeana felt like she was going crazy. But at least the woman didn't actually grope her. The psychological pressure Deeana was under was enormous. She said it was like being in prison where she had to be somebody's punk just to be protected.

Finally she couldn't stand being grabbed by the man and filed a sexual harassment complaint. At the hearing, his military lawyer pointed out that she had no witnesses to back up any of her claims. He listed all the disciplinary reports the sergeant had filed on her and said her harassment complaint was just her way of getting even with him for reporting her bad behavior.

The board denied her complaint but said they would transfer her to separate the two of them. Deeana got orders for Iraq.

Even if there had been time to file a CO application, it would've almost certainly been denied. Jane made a few calls to ecumenical colleagues in the Catholic Church in Venezuela. Deeana went on leave to Mexico and never came back.

We got a letter for her recently saying she likes Venezuela. She's working as a desk clerk at an international hotel and is glad to be free.

— 5—

Generations

A Granny for Peace told of finding young allies in the struggle against military recruiting.

It's never easy being a parent or a child. The generations always have friction between them, a conflict between the elders' need to give guidance and the youths' need to find their own way. I grew up in the 1950s, when the USA was very conservative and bound by traditions. My parents' generation had grown up in the Depression amid poverty and then struggled through World War Two with its threat of death and destruction. By the time they were ready to start families, they were fixated on stability and security. They measured their progress by their possessions: buying their first car, first television, first house. Their morality centered on controlling sexuality and protecting private property. Their religion was a death cult of stern patriarchs, obedient virgins, innocent babies, and threats of eternal torture. Their deepest philosophy was "There is no free lunch." The peak of their scientific achievement was the hydrogen bomb. Fear was their strongest emotion.

I was raised in an ethos of striving for money. My parents were landlords. With the help of a small inheritance of my mother's and my father's unionized factory job, they'd bought a duplex house on a long mortgage. They rented the other half out, scrimped and saved, and were able to get another mortgage on a rundown four-unit apartment building. They worked every weekend fixing it up, and in a few years had enough equity to buy another building. My dad was able to quit his factory job and devote full time to property management. The more money he made, the harder he worked — it was a drug. He and my mother were always fixing places up, showing them to prospective tenants, shopping for new properties, and fighting with tenants over rent raises. They ran on coffee and tranquilizers and were always exhausted. Dad had ulcers and mom had psoriasis.

By the time I was in high school, we lived in a great big house and they owned a dozen buildings filled with factory workers like he'd once been. He said they could all have what we had if they weren't so lazy. Conveniently forgetting the inheritance that had given us the initial advantage, he was now the American dream of the self-made man.

That's when my parents and I started getting into fights. I couldn't articulate my feelings about the situation, so they came out as sullenness, but what I sensed was that dad and mom had sacrificed everything for money and now that was all they had and it wasn't worth it. The money itself came from the tenants — where else? The high rent those people paid kept them poor, locked them onto the proletarian treadmill with their labor generating prosperity for my parents and the factory owners. I didn't think the tenants were lazy. I thought they wanted to do something else besides work all the time. When they saw what wrecks my parents were, who could blame them for not wanting to scramble all their lives to build a real estate empire?

My friends too were having lots of fights with their parents. We were alienated from their values and determined not to end up like them. We'd grown up with financial security, so it meant little to us. We could see how our parents' obsession with material objects, their sexual repression, and their constant anxiety had warped them. We didn't want to pay such a high psychic price for security, so we rebelled. We rejected their morality, their culture, their racism, and their wars. And they fought back bitterly, accusing us of scorning their sacrifices, of trying to destroy the institutions they'd worked so hard to sustain.

And it was true. Destruction was my generation's greatest talent, and we were surrounded by a society that needed destroying. We arrogantly defied their attempts to make us obey and disdained their efforts to preserve the old ways. We dismantled as much as we could: segregation, the draft, chastity, gender roles. In our rage to change, we kicked holes in the walls of a constrictive environment. We didn't break out of this dungeon, but we let fresh air into the stagnant atmosphere we'd inherited.

My parents hoped I would marry a guy with good business sense, and we would take over and expand their properties into a dynasty. They were disappointed when I married a sociology student, but they gave him all sorts of unwanted advice about how once he had a job he could buy and fix up properties in his spare time and rent them out. Chris, my husband, explained how a compulsive drive for money squelches the human psyche and how landlords are a parasitic class in society. They reacted as if they'd been insulted, and I guess they had been. Disappointed that we were rejecting what they most valued, they predicted a life of deprivation for me, a sinking down to the level of their tenants, from which they had worked so hard to escape.

Chris and I became professors (anthropology for me), and although our income isn't high, we have enough.

My parents were delighted when we had a child. They doted on Josh, and he liked being with them. They even put a bumper sticker on their Cadillac: "If we'd known grandchildren were so much fun, we would've had them first!"

My generation expected our kids would finish the job we had started and tear down the social walls, breaking on through to liberation. But our expectations met with as much disappointment as our parents' had. The new generation enjoyed the fresh air we'd provided: creativity, sexual permissiveness, tolerance of diversity, self-expression. They took these values for granted, just as we had with the material security we'd grown up with. Of course some kids weren't this docile and did oppose established power, but they were the exceptions. Most didn't protest. Their main goal was something we paid lip service to, but deep-down distrusted:

enjoying life. Many things displeased them — lower wages, expensive education, shrinking opportunities — but the hard battles needed to overthrow corporate rulership didn't appeal to them. Rather than rebelling, they accepted the well-ventilated dungeon they found themselves in.

Josh is sensitive and caring, a much more easygoing person than I was growing up. But changing the world isn't his priority. In high school he started working for his grandfather, painting and doing odd jobs on the properties. The two of them got along great.

Although Josh is bright, he didn't study particularly hard and stopped his education with a junior college degree, then went to work full-time for his grandfather, moving up into the business side of it. He met a nice girl, and they got married. He didn't have his grandfather's energy and ambition, but he was making a decent salary and had a free place to live, so he was content. He and his wife became gourmet cooks.

I have to admit I was disappointed by his complacency, but I was also thankful that he and his wife were wholesome, not into drugs or self-destructiveness. They were a pleasant, stable family. Their son, Mark, was a delightful boy, and then they had a daughter, Linda, a real dear. I didn't mind baby-sitting at all.

As our grandchildren grew older, my husband and I enjoyed an easy communication with them. By the time Mark was in high school, we were having real intellectual discussions. I didn't have to persuade him to be against the war, he was that way spontaneously.

When the Army set up a recruiting booth in Mark's school, he decided to oppose it with a counter-recruiting booth. This is now legal, thanks to long court battles fought by the peace movement. Grannies for Peace, the American Friends Service Committee, and the War Resisters League — my favorite political organizations — have programs to defend kids against the lies that recruiters use to round up new bodies for the war.

Mark told his school administration he wanted to put a booth next to the Army's. They told him only registered student groups were allowed booths, he couldn't do it as an individual. So he decided to form a club. Finding enough students to join was the easy part; the hard part was clearing all the bureaucratic hurdles the administration put in their way.

Finally Students for Peace was approved and given permission to set up an information table. It couldn't be right next to the Army booth but rather across the hall "to avoid congestion." Linda (she's in junior high now) and I painted banners proclaiming "Not Your Soldier!" and "Recruiters Lie!" and ordered brochures about what to really expect when you join the military and about ways to finance college without enlisting in Murder, Inc.

Josh and his wife were worried their children would turn into troublemakers and were perturbed at me for "egging them on."

The students had the great idea to dress up in Halloween skeleton costumes and to hand out glasses of red cranberry juice that looked like blood. As Mark told me later, the costumes and drinks were a great hit. They totally undermined the "career counseling" the recruiters claimed to be offering, and showed what the military was really about. The two sergeants complained to the principal, who agreed with them that this was unfair. An info table was one thing, but ridicule was going too far. Plus the school dress code didn't include skeleton costumes. Either change clothes and get rid of the cranberry juice, or he'd shut down the table.

Mark and his friends obeyed, but then began singing the Funeral March: "Gone to the morgue, that's the only place for me," just loud enough so people at the recruiting booth could hear. A crowd of students had gathered by then, and a lively open debate was going on about the pros and cons of enlisting. The school has a Junior Reserve Officers Training Corps program, and the members were there in uniform supporting the recruiters. Some of the future officers got upset and frustrated by the debate and turned over the counter-recruiting table.

The principal came back mad and said Students for Peace were causing a disturbance and he was putting a stop to their "publicity stunt." He had the janitor remove the table to the storeroom and ordered all the students to clear the hall.

The next week when the recruiters were due to come back, Mark and his friends asked again to set up a table and said they wouldn't sing. The principal refused, saying they had violated school regulations, and if they pulled anything like this again, he would dissolve the club.

The students met at my house, angry about these repressive tactics. They decided that if they couldn't set up an info table, there wasn't much reason to have a club, so might as well keep protesting even if the club got banned.

I loved these kids — they were so smart, full of spirit, and unintimidated by authority. They were much bolder than I was at that age. But they were also more rash and reckless.

As Mark told me later, they organized a counterattack. One of them found on the Internet instructions for making a stink bomb, some disgusting mix of sulfur, hair, and rubber bands. They got a trash can and painted "Death Stinks" on it, then glued the stink bomb to the bottom of the can. Mark and a friend lit the bomb outside the school door, slapped the lid on the garbage can, and carried it inside, wearing ski masks to hide their faces. In front of the recruiting booth, they pulled the lid off the can, shouting, "Death stinks!" as putrid smoke billowed out.

"Get those guys!" the recruiting sergeant ordered the Junior ROTCs standing next to the booth. Mark and his friend ran out the door, but the ROTCs caught up. Mark tried to ward them off using the garbage can lid as a shield, as if it were a jousting game. But the ROTCs were mostly jocks, tough and mean, and were after blood. They kicked and beat the two boys, pulled off their masks, and held them there until the principal arrived. He suspended the two of them from school for a week but didn't do anything to the others.

Hurt and mad, Mark went home, got a hammer and nails, and returned to school. In the parking lot he found the recruiters' car and pounded a nail into each tire.

He and his friend were arrested for vandalism, malicious mischief, and destroying government property, and were expelled from school. The police told them they had ironclad proof, but if both boys pleaded guilty, they could get off with probation. If they pleaded innocent, though, they'd get at least three months in juvenile hall and their parents would have to pay a five thousand dollar fine. All that time in juvie would mean they'd fail a semester of school and wouldn't graduate with their class.

I visited Mark in the detention center. He was scared by the police threats, but we wondered how they could have proof. He was sure no one had seen him. Even his friend didn't know what Mark had done, but the cops claimed he was part of it. We decided they were probably bluffing to get them to confess.

I hired an attorney, and she urged both boys to plead innocent. The police made more threats but eventually had to drop the charges for lack of evidence.

The principal said they were still expelled from school, so they would fail the semester and not graduate. At this, the lawyer threatened to sue the school. Expulsion is much more serious than suspension and requires evidence. The school backed down and readmitted both boys.

The best news, though, was that the recruiters decided this school wasn't worth the hassles, and stopped setting up their booth. To celebrate the victory, my husband and I took all the Students for Peace out to dinner. They're a great bunch of youngsters. I'm so glad there's a new crop of activists coming up.

Josh and his wife were upset about Mark getting into trouble, worried this would damage his future. To them it was the same as if he'd been arrested for drugs or shoplifting — a black mark on his record. They were angry at me for "putting him up to it."

Their discomfort about defying authorities reminded me of something my father had told me before he died. He confided to me that during the 1930s his father had joined the Communist Party, was arrested several times for agitating, and was fired from his job due to his political activities. Dad was embarrassed to tell me this, as if it was a shameful family secret he had to get off his chest.

I never knew my grandfather, but hearing the story, I very much wished I had. I'll bet we could have related to each other the way I can with Mark and Linda.

— 6 —

Coming Home

A mother tells the story of her soldier son's return from deployment. Because of their illegal activities, neither was willing to be interviewed. I received this account through a mutual acquaintance.

My son spent a year fighting in Afghanistan and Iraq in Delta Force. It was the worst year of his life ... and of mine. As he told me later, there were times he thought he'd never come home. That was also my constant fear. For 365 days, every time the phone rang I thought it would be a voice from the Pentagon telling me with well-practiced condolence that my son had died a hero.

Jim had joined the Army after college. I think he was trying to finally win his father's approval. The old man was a West Pointer who had served a long military career, including two tours in Vietnam, and retired a colonel. He probably would've made general if it hadn't been for his drinking. He never showed much interest in Jim and me, preferring the camaraderie of his soldier buddies.

We divorced when Jim was in high school. The colonel didn't ask for visitation rights, and Jim was crushed when it became obvious that his dad didn't care about seeing him.

Jim and the colonel had little in common. Jim wasn't the military type — he didn't go in for rough sports or violent movies. He was a sensitive boy who liked to read. He and I had similar interests and could communicate well together, much better than most mothers and teenaged sons.

In college Jim majored in English, which dad dismissed as wimpy. Disapproval was the colonel's default setting, and this ate away at Jim for years, undermining his self-confidence.

Although I was dismayed to see Jim following in his father's footsteps by enlisting in the military, dad finally took notice of him. When Jim graduated from Officer Candidate School, dad actually showed some pride and introduced the young lieutenant to his buddies. He spent more time with his son; Jim had finally done something the colonel could identify with.

At last Jim was getting the patriarchal attention he had craved so much when he was younger, and he ate it up. He became more and more like his dad, and I felt left out. My son was now a gung-ho soldier. He was polite with me but distant, awkward, a bit condescending. We couldn't talk together anymore like we used to. He was slipping away, becoming another person, one I didn't feel as comfortable with.

When Jim volunteered for Delta Force, dad was really impressed but I was distraught. By then the "war on terror" (what a false propaganda slogan that is, since war itself is the greatest terror) was underway, and I knew he'd be in the middle of the fighting.

First Jim was in Afghanistan, chasing Osama bin Laden, then in Iraq, chasing Saddam Hussein. These were men the USA had originally helped into power and armed so they could kill Russians and Iranians. When they ungratefully turned against their masters, they became monsters who now needed to be destroyed. In trying to get them, we've killed three hundred thousand people — a hundred times more than were killed in 9/11 — and sown the seeds for far worse terrorism.

The US attacks on Afghanistan and Iraq made it clear that George W. Bush, Saddam Hussein and Osama bin Laden are the same type: violent men who kill to impose their will. Men like this are too primitive to be leaders — they'll kill us all.

My main fear of course was the risk to Jim's own life, but I also hated the thought of him killing other people, and I resented our government for sending him into such violence just for the sake of cheap oil and corporate profits.

I'd never been particularly political before, but what Jim was going through radicalized me. I began to see that the roots of aggression are not just economic but also patriarchal — generations of ruling fathers lusting for war and passing this addiction on to their sons. The sons imitate the fathers because they yearn for their approval. Given this syndrome, as long as men hold the power, they will continue to slaughter each other.

There have of course been a few women warriors and war-mongering women politicians, but they seem to me to be products of patriarchy, women wanting to be men. Most women, as the givers of life, are repelled by killing.

Jim had been repelled by it too when he was younger. Whenever we had mice, he couldn't stand the idea of killing them and insisted on using a live trap so we could let them go outdoors. We cried together for days when we had to have our sick, elderly dog put to sleep. Jim had been kind and gentle, but that was when we were close, before he decided to join the patriarchs.

His military training seemed to have hardened his heart, made him less emotional. What had a year of war done to him? I was afraid of what he might be like when he came home ... if he came home.

I was overjoyed when he finally returned to the States with only a minor wound. He had a month's leave before his next assignment and flew out to visit me.

I hardly recognized him as he came through the flight gate. He was in uniform with a green beret and black hightop boots. He looked older, bigger, harder. But when he scooped me up into his arms for big hug and kiss, I nearly fainted with relief.

I had planned a special celebration with dinner at a fancy restaurant, but he said he'd rather stay home and have a quiet evening here. As I looked at him more closely, he seemed sad and tired.

I pulled all my culinary skills together and cooked him the best meal I could manage. I also laid in a supply of Jack Daniels. It was his father's favorite bourbon and now Jim's ... following in the footsteps.

I was happy he was home safe with me, but I was worried about him being sent back there. This war was not going to end anytime soon.

We had drinks before, during, and after the meal, needing to let go of a year's worth of anxiety. I could tell he was glad to see me, but he was also full of sorrow. Trying to wash away bad memories with alcohol doesn't work very well, and he got gloomier as the evening went on.

I thought a movie might distract him, cheer him up, so I put in a comedy DVD and we sat together on the couch to watch it. Somehow none of the jokes seemed funny, though, and I switched it off.

I decided to try the direct approach. "Jim, tell me about it. Just tell me all about it. Maybe you need to get the war off your chest."

He looked grief-stricken, and I took his hand.

He was silent awhile, then began to speak hesitantly. "I'll try to tell you. Something terrible happened there ... Iraq. Well, lots of terrible things ... but one particular. I shouldn't say 'it happened' ... that's a cop out. I did something ... was part of something. I don't want to talk about it ... but I guess I should. Maybe it'll help." He paused, then said in a strained whisper, "And I know you'll still love me ... no matter what I did," but with a hint of a question in his voice.

I nodded and squeezed his hand but stayed silent so he'd keep talking.

His face collapsed into tears, but he took a deep breath and continued. "There was a car ... coming down the road ... outside of Baghdad. And we ... we had a checkpoint, supposed to stop all the cars ... search them. This car ... didn't stop ... drove off the road to get around us ... just kept going. Our captain yelled, 'Suicide bombers! Get 'em!'"

Jim paused and looked at me, damp eyes full of torment. "The day before ... a car had driven into some Americans, blown them up. We thought they were headed for our main outfit. We shot them up."

He looked away from me, and I could hardly hear him speak. "But there wasn't any bomb ... just two women and four kids ... afraid of us ... just trying to get away from us ... and we killed them ... we killed them all."

A cry broke from him and he doubled over, gasping. Sobs shuddered through his body, and he kept shaking his head as if he couldn't believe, couldn't bear to believe, he'd killed those people. I could tell he'd been carrying this misery around since then, caught in a guilt he couldn't release.

I had to save him from this, but I had no idea how. Acting on instinct, I hugged him to me and saw a helpless need beneath the tears on his face. His head was on my shoulder, and I pulled it down onto my bosom, the place where he'd been totally content and happy. He clutched me and mouthed yearningly at me through my blouse while I stroked his head.

My nipples tightened from stimulation but my chest tightened from fear. Uh-oh, wait, I thought, what's happening here? This is going too far. Stop!

But I couldn't. His need seemed to put me into a trance. I somehow knew this was the only thing that would help him. Unable to refuse him, I let him open my blouse and bra and touch my breasts. He was weeping and whimpering as he kissed them. His tears were streaming on them and his nose was running on them. Finally he stopped crying and his gasps became gurgles. He sucked and licked and gulped at them as if trying to swallow them.

I was in shock. I kept telling myself, *You're his mother ... You're his mother*. At first these words were to get me to stop, then they became the reason to continue. I knew I was the only one who could rescue him now, who had an antidote to the violence. If this would help, that was more important than some old rules about good and bad. I could feel healing love for my son welling up inside me and flowing out my breasts into him. I ran my fingers through his hair to let him know it was all right.

When he had nursed enough, he sought my mouth, his eyes closed but no longer crying. We kissed in a fusion of giving and need. I was giving everything I had to comfort him, and he was taking it, and it was helping. I've never been kissed with such desperation, but it was calming him — I could feel his trauma lessening.

As he embraced me, the medals on his uniformed chest poked my breast. "Ow!" I protested, drawing back. "Those things ... hard and cold."

"Sorry," he said with a wince and stroked the breast to make the pain go away. Our eyes met in chaos: *What were we doing? Were we really going to do this? Incest! No!*

Jim looked down at the medals that had hurt me. "Get rid of these things." he said, tearing off his shirt.

I saw a spray of pink welts across his chest, scars from grenade shrapnel where he'd been wounded. "Does it still hurt?" I asked.

He shook his head, no.

I touched the scars delicately, tentatively, wishing I could make them disappear. Jim was my little boy and he was a grown wounded man. I got rid of the rest of my blouse and bra, and our bare chests joined. I pressed my breasts against his scars, trying to bring back some softness to his life. Eyes closed to shut off our minds, we went back to kissing and rubbing against each other.

Before, it had been more comforting, a maternal soothing of pain, but now it became more sexual, a man and woman wanting each other. I let him do whatever he wanted ... and he wanted it all, right there on the couch, then on the rug. He broke the zipper of my skirt getting it off. He had a terrible time taking off his hightop paratrooper boots. Once nude, we took one look at each other and closed our eyes again, afraid eye contact would make us stop.

It was all too urgent for foreplay. As my son entered me, I tried to envelop him with total love and acceptance, to drive away the memories that were torturing him. I embraced him with my arms, my legs, every part of my body, and he needed everything I could give. I've never felt so needed.

As he cried out this time, it was a cry of joy.

He fell asleep right afterwards, and I lay beside him, watching him. As his face relaxed, the strain that had tightened it before faded away, leaving it clear and young again.

I was happy and mortified at the same time. Why had I done this? My heart said it was right, but my head said it was wrong. I tried to sort out a storm of conflict.

Intuitively I knew I was giving him a way out of the violence. Unless I broke him out of his torment, only two paths would be left for him: He'd either repress what he'd done in Iraq and become an unfeeling brute, or be overwhelmed by it and destroy himself.

I was offering him the opposite of the military mentality. I was taking my son back from those savage men who run the world, winning him away from the warriors.

I woke him up enough to get him into my bed, then fell asleep beside him knowing what we'd done was right.

In the gray hangover morning, though, things looked different. We were both groggy, headachy, aghast at last night. Had we actually done that — crossed the great divide that separates mothers and sons? What would happen to us now?

Barely looking at me, Jim scooted out of bed wrapped in a sheet, and we showered in separate bathrooms. Over coffee he said with a contrite, self-blaming shake of his head, "I'm really sorry ... about what happened. I don't know what got into me."

Looking at his bleak expression, I knew if he added this to his load of guilt, it would crush him. He was balanced between condemnation and love, and I had to tip him in the life-affirming direction. I took his hand and tried to break through his regrets with my eyes. "Jim, please believe me, it was wonderful. I'm so glad you made love to me."

I began to cry; he moved his chair next to mine and held me in his arms. "Don't think it was wrong. It was right ... it was the best thing!" I insisted and kissed him passionately on the lips. He kissed me back. I stroked his face and head, he stroked me. I rubbed my breasts against him; he breathed deeply and took both of them in his hands. Now desire had replaced guilt on his face. We stood up without a word, and I led him back to bed.

Making love with your son first thing in the morning turns out to be a great hangover cure!

For him really to leave the past behind, we needed a change of place, a new setting for our new development, so we drove to the coast and stayed at a lodge by the sea. It turned into a honeymoon. We made love on the beach among driftwood logs. We made love driving back from dinner, pulling off the road and diving into the rear seat because we couldn't wait until we got to our room. We made love on the deck of a small sailboat and nearly capsized. We made love!

At first we didn't talk of the war — just blotted it out with positive experiences, replaced it with affection. Our talk was about each other and the beautiful nature around us.

After a week we returned home, and Jim shared my bedroom. We enjoyed the most wonderful rapport. During the day, he worked on the house — fixing things, cleaning out the attic, getting the storm shutters ready for winter. At night, we snuggled together.

Gradually we talked more about the war. We worked a lot on forgiveness, getting him to stop blaming himself, to lift the guilt from his broad shoulders.

I left a book by Noam Chomsky prominently on the coffee table, and Jim picked it up and began reading. He was shocked to learn that in every nation where we now have terrorism, the USA had first done terrible things. We've overthrown their governments, installed dictators, undermined their economies — all to strengthen our business interests. The terror attacks are retaliation for what we've done to their countries.

Chomsky shows how our corporate media have created an image of fiendish terrorists who "hate us for our freedom." But they really hate us for dominating them. Since we started the aggression, the attacks, detestable as they are, won't end until we change our policies.

The most pathetic thing is that we Americans still believe it's "our" country, when it and both political parties are firmly in the hands of the corporations.

Jim and I talked and talked, sometimes argued, about these issues. This view went against everything he — and all of us — had been raised to believe. We've all been subjected as children to patriotic rituals that caused us to connect the nation we live in with our family and then with God — the founding fathers, our own father, and the Heavenly Father all joined in patriarchy. Because of this emotional identification, we react to criticism of the country as an attack on our family. This hurts our feelings on a deep personal level, so we reject it, convinced it can't be true. It's too threatening to us. We tune it out and often resent the people making it.

But Jim's war experience showed that the criticism he was reading was true. As he and I connected what he'd read with the things he'd seen, he began to question his military obedience. Gradually he came to oppose this "war on terror," then all war and killing. This was a painful transition for him: It meant turning against his father.

At the end of his leave time, he went to the Pentagon and resigned his Army commission. When he told his father this, the old man yelled he was disowning him and hung up the phone. Jim has tried to communicate a couple of times since then, but dad won't talk to him.

That was months ago. Jim and I are still close, but we're not living together. He's in graduate school, working on a PhD in peace studies, an interdisciplinary program involving anthropology, psychology, economics, political science, theology, and philosophy. He's determined to use his experiences to convince others to reject the military and resist war.

— 7 —

From Cheerleader to Enemy of the State

The long, flouncy curls from Judy Davis's cheerleader days are gone. Her straight blonde hair is now cut short. Large blue eyes stand out in a face pale without makeup. Her soft Southern drawl has an undertone of determination. "It's taken me a while, but now I'm glad to be considered an 'unsuitable influence.' That was how the school board justified my firing. That and 'deviating from the curriculum.' It's like they were implying I was a deviant. And according to their norms, I am."

The twenty-nine-year-old was fired for teaching her high school students how US foreign policy has provoked terrorism. This struggle with her school board turned her from a Republican into a revolutionary for peace.

"I taught my tenth grade American history class about what the USA has done for decades in the countries in which we now have terrorism. We work with the local oligarchs there to keep the country under control for our economic advantage. We support dictators and also the kind of managed democracy we have in the USA, where the only political parties that have a chance are those aligned with business and the private ownership of resources. People in those countries are tired of being kept at the bottom. They're tired of CIA coups and assassinations of progressive leaders. So now they're defending themselves the only way they can. And they're getting pretty good at it.

"This was a lesson for my class in history, but also in cause and effect, as I explained what has provoked so many people to such anger at the USA. But the effect on me was that I got fired and am now apparently blacklisted.

"One of the students had an uncle stationed in Iraq, and she reacted as if I had insulted him. She took it as an attack on her family.

"I reminded her that I wasn't criticizing our soldiers but the government's reasons for sending them there. I wanted very much for her uncle to return safely home. But she insisted I had no business saying any of that.

"That led to a mini-lesson on freedom of speech in which the whole class took part. It was one of the liveliest but also most emotionally charged discussions we'd had. Several students were convinced what I had said were lies, and freedom of speech doesn't include the right to lie. They denied the USA had harmed these countries. They insisted the terrorists are maniacs who hate us for our freedom, hate us because we're Christian. We have to stop them before they kill us.

"While we were talking, I looked in the corner at the American flag, with its red for the blood of our brave soldiers. Every morning the students put their hands over their hearts and pledge allegiance to that flag in a ritual designed to evoke tender feelings of identification with our country. I saw the portraits of the Founding Fathers on the walls, all looking so wise and kind, just the father every child would like to have. I thought about all the patriotic civics classes that teach us how great America is but leave out much of our history, particularly foreign policy.

"I realized these kids — all of us — are being indoctrinated, not just by the schools but also by the press and entertainment. Rather than thinking critically, we're encouraged to react emotionally. One of the media's purposes is to keep our emotions stirred up so we don't think too much.

"Several students took my side, but for some of them that was because I was the teacher, the authority figure. But others had really thought about the issue and added ideas of their own that had never occurred to me. One African-American girl made brilliant connections between the kind of invisible colonialism the USA tries to enforce on other countries and its domestic colonization of poor minority groups here.

"The discussion was an intense learning experience for us all. Its goal wasn't to try to change opinions but to clarify what we really believe and help us articulate that. We all benefited from it.

"Next day the principal called me in because of student complaints. My explanations didn't convince her, but she indicated if I apologized to the class and never did anything like this again, she could let the incident slide.

"When I refused, she said she'd have to bring the matter before the school board. The board — made up of business leaders, a minister, and a retired educator — interviewed me and issued a report saying my 'inappropriate behavior and recalcitrant defense of it' left them no choice but to dismiss me.

"Previous to this, my professional evaluations had always been excellent. Since the firing, I've applied for other jobs in the state and haven't got one interview. And there's a shortage of teachers in the state."

Judy and I were talking in the cramped living-dining-room-kitchen of the rental trailer she had to move into after being fired. The air conditioner was broken, and the room was hot and humid. I was grateful for the iced tea with a sprig of mint.

She showed me her photos as a high school and college cheerleader, full of pep and team spirit. Now she was embarrassed by them.

"I can look back and see how I was serving a ritual designed to make young people identify with their school and its team, cheering it on to victory over the other team. School sports are sort of trainer wheels to prepare us for military patriotism. We cheer our athletes, then we cheer our troops. Our group is naturally the special good one who deserves to win. It's interesting that George W. Bush was a cheerleader.

"But at the time I got fired, I hadn't thought of any of that. I was just examining the history of US involvement in the Mideast.

"I wasn't radical. My parents voted Republican, and I had followed their lead. But those days are over.

"The whole incident made it clear to me how much thought control goes on in our society, how mentally manipulating the media and the educational institutions are.

"After being fired I had lots of free time, so I read books by Naomi Klein, William Blum and Howard Zinn. I learned more about how the power holders use patriotism to quash dissent and make the people afraid of outside enemies. I learned how the global rich act in their own interests regardless of nationality, and how this keeps the majority of the world in poverty. We're not going to have peace until we stop this.

"Now I'm a waitress in a chain restaurant. That's been a good lesson in capitalism. I'm making a lot less money, but the government still takes a hefty chunk of it to kill people they think are a threat to them."

When I asked Judy what she was doing to stop that, she gestured self-mockingly at her petite form and said, "Believe it or not, this person, all 105 pounds of me, has become an enemy of the state. I'm actively working to bring it down, particularly the patriarchal, capitalist form that we live under."

"That's a big assignment," I said. "How do you think we can build something different?"

"Well, we first have to realize the men in charge aren't going to let us build anything really different," she replied. "They'll do everything they can, no matter how vicious, to hold on to power. And they've got too many on their side now.

"I think our job is to clear the ground so something new *can* be built. We have to weaken this monolith so it will eventually fall, undermine it, chip away at it however we can. That's probably going to be a lifetime assignment for us. The generations who come after us can decide what to build in its place. That's their job, and it's presumptuous of us to try to do that for them.

"Planning a new society at this point seems to me to be just daydreaming, spinning fantasies. First we have to break this system's power. Otherwise our descendants will still be living under it."

I objected that this sounds pessimistic, but she didn't agree.

"I'd call it realistic," she countered. "It's clear by now that this system is not going to allow basic changes. Only superficial reforms come out of Congress, and they're often reversed later on.

"Both major parties are tied to the business establishment, which wields the real power. The Democrats tolerate occasional eccentrics like Dennis Kucinich to create an impression of progress, but they don't have a chance of achieving power. The establishment uses them to channel public discontent into dead-end streets, to convince people if they wait another four years, this system could change. But it never does. Liberalism's purpose is to maintain the power structure by stringing people's hopes along to the next meaningless election.

"It's so much more comforting to believe things will improve someday and that the system is mostly fair, just has a few problems. And from the top half of society it looks that way. But from the bottom half, especially overseas, it looks quite different. And that's where the changes are going to come from, not from the liberals."

"What do you see happening?" I asked her.

"Guerrilla warfare will gradually defeat the empire overseas, prevent it from expanding. So it'll turn inward and start squeezing its own people more. Since it's inherently unjust, that's the only way it can maintain itself. When we revolt against that, it'll turn fascist. In a couple of generations we'll overthrow the fascism. And then we'll build ... who knows? That's a long ways away, and we have a lot to do until then."

"That seems depressing," I said.

"No! What we have now is depressing. Overthrowing it will be a great adventure. Resistance is energizing. That's what liberation is about."

"What would you suggest doing?" I asked.

"Direct action. There are all sorts of nonviolent ways to undermine power. Depriving the corporations and their government of money is a good start. This can be done by work sabotage, by tax evasion, by refusing to buy things. Consumer strikes are particularly important for women because the media are continually screaming at you to get new stuff. That's how you're supposed to get rid of the feelings of inadequacy that patriarchy has instilled in you — grab the latest clothes, hairstyles, makeup, furnishings so you can feel better about yourself. But if you just stop obeying them, stop buying that crap, use the old stuff until it wears out, defy the image makers, then you liberate yourself from this sick culture. That's when you can really start feeling good about yourself.

"For one thing, you're de-financing the war. Corporate and government resources are limited. Every dollar less that you give them is one they can't give to the military.

"This war has already devastated the economy. Taxes and the national debt are maxed out. They can't go higher. If costs continue to rise and we continue to lose, the only solution will be to pull out the troops. Mass murder has become a luxury the USA can no longer afford. Thousands of small acts of citizen sabotage will help pull the plug on the war.

"Making concrete suggestions about this could get me put in jail these days, so I can't be too specific. But each of us has gifts for resistance, and I think we should use them to toss monkey wrenches into the works. I have a few personal projects that mean a lot to me.

"Most Americans object to this approach because it might affect their personal lives. We've been brought up to see that as our top priority. But allowing our government to be viciously militaristic will inevitably harm our lives more. To end the cycle, we have to stop the killing, even if that temporarily makes things harder for us. The two forms of aggression — wars abroad and declining wages at home — are linked. Both are functions of capitalism. We need to break its hold on us."

Beneath the bravado, her voice was now tinged with anxiety. She didn't want to say too much. She didn't know me very well. She — like all of us — wasn't sure how far her freedoms go anymore.

"Doing something as mild as voting for a minor party deprives the major parties of votes and shows how illegitimate they are."

"What if that helps someone like Bush get elected?" I wanted to know.

With a dismissing wave she said, "I think this idea that Bush is the problem is a red herring. It's used to distract us from the fact that US militarism has bipartisan support. It helps perpetuate the system by focusing on personalities rather than policies. Bush's crudeness just made more clear what US policy has been for over two hundred years: empire building. The other presidents just did it less blatantly.

"Thomas Jefferson was the founding father of imperialism. He said we should move in to replace the fading power of the Spanish empire in Latin America. And we've done that, sometimes by conquest, sometimes by working through their local rulers.

"The founding fathers were just rich men looking after their own interests. Just like our current leaders are. We need to knock these patriarchs off their pedestals.

"They've become masters at recruiting women to serve their interests. Most women politicians are offering us the same old system dressed up in a new outfit, just patriarchy with perfume."

I asked her how she thinks we should oppose patriarchy.

With a mix of irony and sincerity that showed her to be both a radical feminist and a well-mannered Southern lady, she first asked me if I would like more iced tea. Then she said, "Both men and women have internalized patriarchal assumptions, and we've been brought up to think that's the only way things can be. We need to root these implanted concepts out of us. Art can do that. Lesbian and gay cultures can do that. Some psychotherapies can do it. Theologies that oppose the notion of a Heavenly Father can do it.

"Patriarchy has robbed women of our power. That's why so many of us feel incomplete and inadequate. The culture tells us we need a man to fill that void, but we gradually and painfully learn that this traps us in dependency. It isn't fair to the men either, because we've given them the responsibility for making us whole, which is something another person can't do for you. This romantic myth we're fed is like a drug to keep us helpless — "the opiate of the lasses." What we need is not a man. We need to take our power back. Then we can have an equal relationship with a man, if that's what we want.

"At some point opposing patriarchy almost always brings us into opposition to our fathers, and that's scary ground for a lot of us. Before women can change, we have to confront the part of ourselves that still needs our fathers' praise. As long as we unconsciously want to be daddy's little girl, we're going to support the system."

I commented that it sounds like she's got over that.

She shook her head. "I'm still working on it, and it's painful. But you know what? I actually have a better relationship with my father because of it. Now I know him more as an actual person, rather than the projection of an internalized myth. But that too has been a long process."

I said, "None of this — the political and personal change — is easy, is it?"

"No," she concluded, "it's not. But it's worth doing. It's necessary. Things can't go on this way. We can't let business run the world. We can't let governments keep killing people."

— 8 —

Keep On Rockin'

An American exchange student wrote the following essay in one of my courses here in Germany.

Jason was my boyfriend for a while in high school. It wasn't a match made in heaven. Looking back, I think the main thing we had in common was that I wanted a boyfriend and he wanted a girlfriend. Other than that there wasn't much between us, as we discovered whenever we tried to talk about anything. I broke up with him when he asked me to go rabbit hunting with him. We stayed friends, though, probably because it was obvious we could never be a real couple, and neither of us had hard feelings.

We both left town after graduation; I went to college, Jason went to the Marines. Two years later we were both back home; I was on summer vacation, Jason was on medical leave after having half his leg blown off in Iraq. He'd been riding in a truck that hit a mine.

Everybody in town felt terrible about what had happened to him. The American Legion post gave him a parade. The high school marching band played, the vets marched, and Jason walked in front next to the mayor, who was carrying the American flag. Jason could walk pretty well, considering.

They marched into the football stadium, where a couple of hundred people, including me, were sitting in the bleachers. They mayor, the high school principal, and Jason's minister all gave speeches that praised his heroism and the sacrifice he'd made for our freedom. Jason gave a speech about how much he loved his country and how much he appreciated everyone for their support. He said he had a new dream in life. In high school he'd been on the track team, had run the 220. Now he was going to try out for the Special Olympics, to show the world that people can overcome any handicap.

At this, everyone jumped to their feet and gave him a standing ovation. People were crying while they clapped. Jason started to cry, and the minister led him back to his seat. I left the stadium crying while the band played the "Marine Hymn" and "America, the Beautiful."

Some of the people in our class were going to give him a party that night, and I'd been planning to go. But now I kept hearing his voice as he was speaking. It sounded like a machine, like he was saying what everybody wanted to hear and what he wanted to hear, what he wanted desperately to believe but couldn't quite, but if he forced himself to say it and saw everyone else believed it, he might convince himself. Because otherwise it was too terrible, and he couldn't bear that. To block out his grief, Jason had become a robot of patriotism.

I couldn't go to the party and hear him talking in that mechanical voice. I didn't want to hang around home either and hear my parents say how brave Jason was. I poured a little from each of my parents' liquor bottles — bourbon, scotch, vodka, gin, rum, and Southern Comfort — into a jar, then poured in some Coke. Tasted terrible.

I drove my moped down to the river and sat on the bank as it got dark, drinking and watching the slow brown water and listening to the cicadas and frogs chirping like those speeches. I started out sad and then got mad.

I didn't think Jason had been defending anybody's freedom. I drank some more and realized the word "freedom" has become meaningless. It's just a gesture like waving the flag or playing the national anthem to create a feeling in people.

I threw some rocks into the river. I liked the way they splashed but was afraid I might hit a fish.

I got afraid of being out there alone, so I drove away. The strip mall on the edge of town was closed for the night. I saw the Army recruiting office and thought of all the Jasons they're still convincing to sign up and get their legs blown off. I thought it would be more efficient to put the recruiting office, the hospital, and the funeral home all together, so you could just go from one to the next.

I looked around to see if anybody was there. Nobody. I drove to the edge of the parking lot and picked up a big rock. Drove back and when no cars were going by, I threw the rock through the window.

Crashing glass. Wailing alarm. The cardboard dummies of smiling soldiers in the window display fell over. I felt like David knocking over Goliath. But only for a second. Then I got terrified. The cops would be coming. What if my fingerprints were on the rock? What if somebody saw me? I sped away, taking side streets back into town.

I got home OK. My parents were in bed. I threw up in the toilet and went to bed.

Next morning I woke up hung over and afraid. What should I do if police come to the house? Don't admit anything. Maybe they can't prove it.

The newspaper had an article about it and an editorial saying vandalism like this is an insult to Jason and all the other heroes who have sacrificed to defend the free world.

I couldn't resist returning to the scene of the crime. I left the moped a few blocks away in case anyone recognized it, and I wore a hat and sunglasses. The window was covered with a big sheet of plywood, and people were looking at it and talking. I wondered what they were saying but didn't want to get that close.

Over the next several days a stream of letters came out in the paper. Some said people who do things like that should be sent to Iraq. But I was surprised by how many said the war is wrong and we shouldn't be sending our young people over there to fight. It was a real debate that wouldn't have happened unless I'd thrown the rock.

I thought maybe Jason would write a letter, but he didn't. I thought about calling him, but I knew I couldn't say the kind of things that would make him feel better. So I went back to college early.

That town has a recruiting office too, and every time I went by it, I wanted to break the window. But I was too afraid.

Now I'm doing my junior year abroad in Germany. When I read about how the people here who resisted fascism when it was taking over are now honored but back then were despised and persecuted, it made me glad for what I'd done and convinced me I should keep doing it, be careful but take that chance of getting caught. I don't have a police record, so if I did get arrested I probably wouldn't go to prison. It's just breaking a window. Throwing that rock lets people know we can fight back against this, we aren't helpless. Each boarded recruiting window makes people wonder if this war is right, especially if they're thinking of going inside and signing up. And the money it costs the government to fix it can't be used to kill people.

Actually, now that I think about it, it's more than just breaking a window. It's also smashing the glass walls that surround us. This prison we all live in is invisible, but it holds us down. Its walls say, "This is how things have to be, and you have to obey.... These are your only choices.... This is freedom."

The easier a person has it in this society, the harder it is to see it's really a prison for all of us. Even the people at the top have had to sacrifice their humanity to get there and stay there.

Breaking windows doesn't demolish the prison, but it does let in a breath of fresh air, and that makes us yearn for more. It's air conditioning for the brain. Breaking glass is making music. It's do-it-yourself redecoration of our neighborhood. It opens our eyes and lets us see. Breaking glass should be a new Olympic sport ... especially for the Special Olympics.

— 9 —

The Surge

After getting his college degree, a former student of mine worked as a market researcher and an advertising salesperson, but both jobs soured him on the corporate world. He hated being a junior suit, and the thought of becoming a senior suit was even worse.

He's now a janitor and says it's a much better job. He's left alone, it's low pressure, and what he does improves the world rather than worsens it. The pay's lousy but that's standard these days. He loves music, so he loads up his MP3 and grooves to the sounds. Although the work is routine, it's brightened by occasional bits of human interest: used condoms in executive wastebaskets, marijuana butts in the emergency stairwell, a twenty-dollar bill under a desk. His shift is from 6 p.m. to 2 a.m., and afterwards he hits the late-night clubs, where he can enjoy the scene with the advantage of being sober. He works for a janitorial service company, and one of their clients is a defense contractor — not secret weapons, just ordinary supplies.

The man is a pacifist. Originally he felt that rallies, petitions, marches, and picketing would help turn public opinion against the war, and when the majority of Americans opposed it, our political representatives would vote to stop it. That's what democracy means. The first part turned out to be true. Polls showed a clear majority of Americans wanted the war ended and our troops brought home. In 2006 they elected Democratic majorities in the House and Senate who said they would do this. But rather than bringing the soldiers home, "our" representatives voted more money for the war so more soldiers could be sent to Iraq, a surge of troops for another attempt to crush the resistance there. Several months later they voted additional billions for a US troop surge to Afghanistan.

In 2008 the people elected Barack Obama on a pledge to bring peace. But the war still continues with thousands dying, despite the will of the voters to end it.

He began to realize the politicians aren't representing us but what he calls the corpses, short for corporations. The majority of those want the war to continue. It's the corporate majority that rules, not the citizens. That's the democracy we have. When business leaders turn against the war, then it will end.

What would make them turn against it? When they stop making a profit from it, he concluded.

Finally feeling glad to be part of the corporate world, he decided to stage a surge for peace. He bought a 10-amp step-up transformer at an electronics flea market, the kind used to increase voltage from 110 to 220. Next time he was scheduled to work at the defense contractor and the weatherman predicted a thunder storm, he brought the transformer along in his dinner box. At the first flash of lightning, he took it to the data processing center. First he unplugged all the computers and auxiliaries from the surge protectors and zapped them with 220. Then he plugged them back in and zapped the surge protectors. A clear case of surge-protector failure: The damned things must've let the surge through before they shut down.

The stench of sizzled electronics gave him a headache, but other than that he felt fine. He figured the lost work and ruined equipment put a hefty dent in profits. The company will try to pass those costs on to the government, but with budget deficits and taxes already cripplingly high, Congress will finally have to admit they don't have enough money to conquer Iraq and Afghanistan.

The lost work also cuts into the military supply line. If supplies are reduced, war operations have to be reduced.

Soldiers can't fight without logistics. Both economically and tactically, destroying war supplies helps to end war.

He's aware that direct action like this is unpopular. Many people are afraid of government repression that will make their already difficult situation even more unpleasant. But he's convinced that their difficult situation — working long hours for low pay, living in a deteriorating society, raising children amid fear and hostility — is caused by the same forces that drove us to war. Capitalism manifests as invasion in Iraq and Afghanistan, as privatization and impoverishment in Latin America, and as the destruction of the middle class in the industrial nations. It's the same system operating in different environments.

Rather than sheepishly obeying in hopes of avoiding more punishment, he feels we must actively rebel and seize the power that has been usurped from us. This struggle won't be comfortable, but it will be meaningful. By taking charge of our history, we'll earn the gratitude of future generations. Otherwise our and their lives will be continually constricted by the rule of capital. He's convinced the time is ripe for change, and it needs to be fundamental, not superficial.

He grew up in a small town where his family owned the local hardware store. When he was in high school, Wal-Mart moved to town. Their family store couldn't compete with Wal-Mart and went broke. His father became a clerk in the Wal-Mart hardware department at a wage less that what he had paid his lowest employee. Soon he was joined there by the former owners of the local clothing, appliance, sporting goods, and toy stores, all of which had gone broke. Despite their expertise, none was hired as a department manager ... all clerks, because they might harbor resentment. The managers were long-term Wal-Mart employees brought in from outside.

But it wasn't just Wal-Mart that used economics of scale to destroy home-grown businesses. Many farmers in the area had to sell out to corporate agriculture. Local restaurants were replaced by cheaper chains. The real estate office was driven out by a discount franchise. And all the workers were making much less than before. The whole town, except for a few big new houses, became bleak.

His parents had enough money saved so he could go to college with the help of student loans and part-time jobs. But his younger brother and sister couldn't. The brother went into the Navy, where he wouldn't have to actually fight, and the sister worked at Wal-Mart.

What's happening to small businesses in the USA is happening to small countries overseas. Their economies are getting taken over, sucked into the maw of transnational corporations. The World Bank and International Monetary Fund are economic weapons in this conquest. Countries that resist face other weapons, from CIA subversion to outright invasion. Feudalism has been revived and globalized. The nobility are the corporate rulers, the yeomen are their declining ranks of employees, and the serfs are the rest of us worldwide — the huge majority.

He's certain that we're not going to change this system without a fight, and we'd better start now while we still have some freedoms. Hoping to make basic changes through liberal reform is a delusion. We cling to that hope because we've been raised with the comforting myth that we live in a democracy. But behind the "we, the people" rhetoric lies entrenched power determined to maintain itself. The rulers are willing to change only in ways that make more profit, such as expanding the labor pool to include women and blacks, thus enabling them to reduce wages.

The "have a nice life" days are over in the USA. Conditions are getting inexorably worse. Americans are beginning to get the same treatment as people in the client states. As protest to this grows, the power elite will try to crush it. They'll scapegoat the radicals, blaming them for the problems, trying to make them the target of rising populist anger. But dissidents aren't causing these conditions, they're resisting them. The conditions are caused by capitalism's drive to turn the middle class into a white-collar proletariat.

In opposing this process, he's a pacifist but not a passivist. He fights, but only in ways that don't injure living creatures.

Currently his transformer is stowed away, awaiting the next weather report when he can transform more war computers into peaceful scrap.

— 10 —

Saboteur

A government that commits crimes against humanity can't expect to have a law-abiding populace. After the genocide of the Native-Americans, slavery, racism, massive social inequality, imperialist wars, and environmental destruction, criminality now seems normality.

But when the people follow the example of their leaders and commit crimes, they are punished with long prison sentences. The USA incarcerates a far higher proportion of its population than any other country, and we strip felons of the right to vote. The media create a repulsive image of criminals with lurid stories of their despicable deeds. So it's no wonder that most progressive people shy away from illegal protest. Crime is a stigma and the penalties severe.

Legal protest, however, has become increasingly ineffective. It's ignored or misrepresented in the press, and it has negligible political impact, since both major parties are committed to expanding the empire.

The need for new tactics is drawing more activists to direct attacks on state power. This upsets moderates who accept civil disobedience but not sabotage. Radicals argue that these laws enforce an unjust social system and breaking them is necessary for breaking that system's power. Moderates argue that criminality alienates mainstream support and makes activists disreputable.

Expressing the radical position, William Pepper wrote in *An Act of State*, "The root and branch transformation of our society, which is about the shaking up of all the old foundations, will require nothing less than a struggle in whatever focus it ultimately takes against the familiar, the comfortable, the acceptable values and inclinations which constitute a very real type of determinism for each one of us."

Walt Whitman, a radical from way back, phrased this need to break out of old frameworks more poetically: "Unscrew the locks from the doors! Unscrew the doors themselves from their jambs!"

John Sinclair, revolutionary rocker and political prisoner, simply proclaimed, "Kick out the jams, motherfuckers!"

No one I've met embodies this wild, rebellious spirit more than the man we'll call Trucker. He's a peace activist turned saboteur who now specializes in burning military vehicles. We first met in 1970 at a rally against the Vietnam War. This was shortly after the National Guard and police had murdered six demonstrators at Kent State and Jackson State, so the mood was extremely tense.

Our demo was going to start on the Berkeley campus and continue with a march down Telegraph Avenue. The city government had denied us a permit to march and called in police reinforcements from Oakland. The Oakland cops had a reputation for brutality (based on their treatment of the black population), and we were expecting an ugly and possibly violent confrontation. Out of fear, many people decided not to march, but others of us argued that marching was now more important than ever. We needed to defy the government's attempts to scare us into silence.

After speeches and music in front of Sproul Hall, we marched off the campus and were met by a wall of police sealing off Telegraph Avenue. Some of our hard-cores in front tried to break through the barrier but were clubbed down. Cops began firing what looked liked shotguns, and people started screaming and running in panic, but it turned out to be tear gas.

A demonstrator wearing a biker helmet, swim goggles, and a cloth around his face picked up a gas canister with gloved hands and hurled it back at the police — a classic scene of a brave individual defying tyranny. Inspired, I pulled off my old green beret that I'd been wearing and used it to protect my hands as I scooped up a hot canister and threw it back where it came from. I thought about all the grenades I'd thrown in Vietnam and felt much better about this one.

The first line of cops, those who were firing, wore gas masks, but those behind didn't, and I felt a surge of triumph seeing them run from their own gas. But the ones in masks kept advancing and firing, looking like robots.

The peace marchers fell back, fleeing down side streets. Agonized from the tear gas, I sank to my knees, hacking convulsively. My eyes were seared, nose and throat raw, skin burning. Through the tears I saw the guy in the biker helmet approaching. He helped me off the street into a doorway and pulled out a first-aid kit. From a squeeze bottle he squirted glycerin water into my eyes and nose, helped me rinse my mouth and throat with regular water from a canteen, then rubbed moist baking soda under my eyes. He was firm but gentle, like a good combat medic. I saw the cloth around his face was a towel wet with vinegar to absorb some of the gas. This man was equipped.

As soon as I could walk better, we straggled away from the scene. The police strategy had worked: The march was broken up, scattered in all directions. We walked down to People's Park, angry, bitter, exhausted.

The park was full, and no cops dared to show, although they and other agents were probably there undercover. Joints were being passed around, and we got high. Smoking grass back then had an innocence to it that it hasn't had since. Cannabis helped us to abandon the death world we saw around us and resurrect our child-selves. Stoned people were learning to play again, singing, blowing giant iridescent soap bubbles, juggling pine cones, tossing Frisbees back and forth. But under it seethed a mood of defiance and rebellion. A statement in *Ramparts* magazine summed up our feelings: "Alienation is when your country is at war and you want the other side to win." But I would have spelled it "a-lie-nation." A group of conga drummers were playing, and their furious, insistent beat seemed to herald a rising tidal wave of protest that would sweep the militarists out of power.

We didn't realize it at the time, but this wasn't the beginning of the wave but its crest, and in the next years it would dwindle down. But this was better than no wave at all. It didn't sink the ship of state, but it did slosh over the deck. And now a new one is rising that may go even higher.

The events of the day bonded Trucker and me as friends, and although our lives took different directions after that, we stayed in touch. Years ago he went totally underground, changing his identity and location, and since then all I've had for him is an e-mail address, through which we held the following interview.

"Why don't you start by telling us why you became a saboteur."

"Well, like Jerry Garcia said, 'What a long, strange trip it's been.' After you went back to New York, I joined an anarchist affinity group, and we worked with the Weather Underground to move demos in the direction of revolt — trashing the headquarters of war corporations, barricading the entrance to the Oakland Army Terminal, throwing rocks at the cops. By then the fuzz had refined their tactics and had special squads that would target the activists, rush into the crowd and grab the hard-cores. They clubbed me, kicked me, punched me, then charged me with assaulting a police officer. I did four months in the Alameda County Jail. Later I found out our group had been infiltrated. One guy who was always pushing us to be violent was actually an agent. He gave them all our plans, even photos of us he'd made with a hidden camera.

"After that I gave up on groups and since then have focused on individual guerrilla insurrection, autonome actions, monkey-wrenching the machine. Especially now with the Patriot Act, that's become the safest way to work. There's a good book, *Leaderless Resistance*, on how to organize that without getting smashed. You can't totally prevent being infiltrated, but you can prevent the agents from knowing much."

"I remember back then you were complaining about all the infiltration, and I thought you were paranoid, but it turned out you were right."

"Yeah, the government took our threat very seriously and did everything they could to smash us. But they couldn't.

"One of the great days of my life was seeing pictures of the last Americans scrambling onto the helicopters on the roof of the embassy in Saigon, running, as John Lennon said, 'like pigs from a gun.'

"Everyone in the peace movement was deliriously happy. We'd finally ended the war."

"I know that a lot of people in the peace movement think they ended the war, but to me that's stealing credit from the Vietnamese. It's an Americentric attitude — 'We're the all-powerful ones' — similar to the attitude of the politicians who thought they could win the war in the first place.

"The Vietnamese won the war by defeating us. Their resistance made it impossible for us to stay there. They chased us out.

"The peace movement helped encourage us to leave, but the necessity of our leaving was the work of the Vietnamese. The peace movement grew only because the Vietnamese were winning. If the USA had been winning, there wouldn't have been mass protests.

"The same thing is happening now. The Iraqi and Afghan resistance fighters are winning the war, and the protests in the USA are a result of that."

"Well, you were on the ground, and your perspective could be more accurate. I'll grant you that. I probably have slipped into some arrogance about this. It was such a bitter struggle. The government came down so hard on us. But maybe we've claimed too much for our efforts.

"Anyway, once the war was finally over, I and lots of other people were totally burnt out. We needed a break, to depressurize. But after a while exhaustion turned to apathy, and many people lost interest in the ongoing struggle.

"I remember when Nixon violated the Paris Peace Agreement by refusing to pay the reparations we'd promised to help Vietnam rebuild their infrastructure and buy medical supplies. Refusing this humanitarian aid was an outrageous, criminal act, and some of us tried to organize a mass protest. We ended up with a hundred people on the steps of the San Francisco County Courthouse. The momentum was gone.

"I too began to focus more on my personal life. I'd met a woman I wanted to build a future with. We were both tired of being poor. Living on the fringe is a struggle, it wears you down. Neither of us wanted to work for the Man and go the yuppie route, and we wanted something with a bit of adventure to it.

"I'd done a little dealing before, but now we got into it in a big way. Just grass and hash, though — natural plants. I never liked hard drugs. Went to Mexico and spent a long time in Michoacán finding a good connection. Not just price and quality, but also good personal vibes.

"We moved to San Diego, and I cut my hair and shaved my beard. Customs was using dogs on the border by then, but we came up with a way to beat that. Formed a little company called Baha Divers, stenciled this on the sides of a van. I'd drive south across the border about every other day with the van full of scuba tanks and gear, supposedly to give diving lessons to the tourists at Rosarito Beach. The US border guards thought of course American tourists would rather learn to dive from an American. In Mexico we sealed the stuff inside the tanks. We filled them with hash because it's more concentrated. I had cut the tanks in the middle and had an airtight way to reseal them. Then we would wash them off with ammonia, to get rid of any smell. The first couple of times I was totally nervous and was afraid the guards would pick up on that, but they didn't. Pretty dull bunch. After a while they didn't even bother to put the dog in the van, just waved me through.

"People I'd known in the Bay area were now spread all over the West Coast, so before long we were supplying all the way up to Vancouver.

"But one day the border guards flagged me into the inspection lane. They knew exactly what they were looking for, took the tanks apart and handcuffed me. It turned out that one of our guys on the Mexican side had got busted by the *Federales*, and he traded his way into a lower sentence by ratting me out.

"It looked bad, like I'd be going back to the Bay area — all the way to San Quentin. But we hired a very good, *very* expensive lawyer, and he got me off. I had to plead guilty as part of a plea bargain but ended up with a suspended sentence.

"After that we switched to boats across the border. The ocean out there is so beautiful. We'd see whales migrating down to their breeding grounds, porpoises playing. Flying fish would land on the deck, we'd toss them back in. Water and sky everywhere. I never knew there were so many different kinds of blue. And the birds and clouds, different whites. All of it moving together but to different rhythms. And we were just a little part of it rocking along.

"We were always tense, though, could never totally relax. That's the trouble with dealing. Coast Guard checked us a couple of times, but we had everything hidden in a lower hull. And plenty of fishing gear and beer as camouflage. After the bust I'd got a new ID, so my name wouldn't get flagged in a routine check.

"Once a gang of Crips highjacked a whole shipment from us at the dock. They had guns and acted like they wanted to use them. Highly unpleasant.

"But they weren't as bad as the Mafia. When the syndicate moved into grass and hash, they made it clear they didn't want competition. They made me an offer I couldn't refuse — a bust or a bullet. If I didn't 'retire,' they'd first set me up for a bust. If that didn't get rid of me, the bullet would.

"I knew other dealers they'd set up on busts. The DEA went along with it because they needed the arrests and because they'd rather do business with the Mafia than with a bunch of hippies. Most of us freelancers wouldn't bribe them like the wise guys did. It sounds funny, but I thought it would be immoral to bribe the police. Selling grass was one thing, but bribing a cop was another. I was actually shocked when I found out a lot of them were taking money.

"I decided to get out while I was ahead ... while I still had a head. By then our savings were enough to buy a spread of land with an old farmhouse in Oregon. We settled down, went back to college, got involved in local issues and environmental organizing.

"Then it all exploded in our faces. We let a guy, friend of a friend, stay with us for a couple of weeks. He was going through hard times and needed some peace and quiet out in the country. He was active in the Black Panthers, and so of course the cops were hassling him, but what we didn't know was that they had warrants on him for the armed robbery of three supermarkets. They tracked him out to our farm and arrested everybody there, charged us all with the robberies. He had some of the loot with him, and he'd given us some bills that turned out to be marked, so that tied us in. Cops found a few pot plants in our garden and added drug charges. They could tell we were radicals, so they wanted to send us away for as long as they could. They had only my new name, but I knew before long they'd match my prints with the California bust, and I'd be looking at major time as a repeat offender.

"We decided to scram. Sold the house and land. Our forfeited bail took a huge chunk of that, but since we weren't going to pay taxes, we came out OK. With the help of some of our old contacts, we transferred the money offshore, then followed it and kept moving, got passports under new names. We thought about staying overseas and becoming ex-pats, but we both missed the USA. The thing is, we like the country. We just don't like the people running it.

"We had some facial surgery — my wife loves her new nose — and after a couple of years came back as different people. We haven't been back to the West Coast, though, don't want to push our luck. And we're super law-abiding, except of course for the small matter of burning military vehicles. We don't even jaywalk.

"Cutting ties was hard. Both our are families are conservative and had shut us out a long time ago, so that part wasn't so difficult. That was pain we'd already gone through. But we had to let go of a lot of friendships. We have webmail with a few close and trusted folks like you, but none of them know where we live or our names."

"Thanks for including me on your list."

"Well, we go back a long time. And those were very formative times.

"But by the time we came back, the country was deep into the Big Chill. Straight and retro. Women were abandoning feminism and returning to femininity, joining the Fascinating Womanhood movement. Guys were majoring in business and wearing suits with suspenders like their grandfathers. Bill Gates replaced John Lennon as the generational hero. Disgusting.

"Maybe as part of our trying to fit into the mainstream, we became tamer ourselves. Got married, in church yet. Stopped smoking dope ... pretty much at least.

"Politically, we started thinking that the way to bring change was through the Democrats, gradual reforms. Now we see that was a trap.

"We turned radical again when Clinton ignored the chance for disarmament that the collapse of the Soviet Union offered. He could've turned the end of the Cold War into a new era of peace. Instead he saw the chance for empire and went for it. Modernized the military with high-tech weapons, clamped sanctions on Iraq that led to millions of children dying from lack of medicine, bombed Yugoslavia and built a huge base there. Rather than Communists, the people who opposed the empire were now called terrorists.

"Domestically he declared war on welfare. Thanks to his policies, millions of single mothers were forced away from their children and into crummy, low-paying jobs. Their kids grew up just as poor but much more neglected.

"Underneath the big smile, Clinton was just a loyal servant of the corporations and the military. Both Clintons are masters of giving the impression of working for real change, but it's just show. And Obama is even better at that show than they are.

"The Democratic Party leadership serves the interests of the mercantile side of the business establishment. They support slightly higher wages and unemployment benefits so people will have money to keeping buy stuff. There's nothing wrong with that, but it doesn't go any farther than that. The basic injustice of the system is never challenged. The Democrats just bring mildly expansionist policies to stimulate the economy.

"The Republicans bring mildly contractive policies that serve the interests of the fiscal side of business. They keep wages low, which holds costs and inflation down and thus preserves the value of capital.

"Although these two tendencies conflict, they're two complementary ways that corporations maintain their control over us, two sides of the same gold coin. Both are necessary for them, and trading the power back and forth keeps things running in a wobbly balance.

"The goal of both parties is to continue this system with little changes here and there, fine tuning. Neither one is going to take it apart and rebuild it, which is what we need. And both parties support an aggressive foreign policy to force US economic and military power into other countries, which is what nobody needs except the corporations they represent.

"Although there's little difference in their policies, there's a great deal of difference in how the parties are marketed to us. Liberal candidates are sold as figures of great hope. We're supposed to think, Finally someone who'll change things. But their changes turn out to be trivial. The system stays mostly the same, and we slump back into disappointment. As the disappointment builds to mass discontent, another fresh liberal face is presented to us with new slogans. But they're all tied to the system. The only candidates that have a chance of getting nominated are those supported by business. They're in their pockets. That's the price of their coming to power.

"Look back in the past. The only major changes to come out of Congress have been the New Deal in the 1930s, passed to stave off a total economic collapse, and the Civil Rights Act in the 1960s, passed under the threat of armed insurrection. And Congress has been whittling away at them ever since.

"We have to take the power away from both parties, close down their whole show. Or else we'll keep on being their vassals.

"We fall for their shell game because we have a desperate need to believe the USA is a great country and our personal lives will turn out well. So we ignore what our leaders are doing in the rest of the world and cling to their mirage of a better future. That's comforting. But things are not improving, they're declining. And that'll continue until we get rid of this corporation government, both parties. We can't build a new system until we break the power of the current one."

"How long do you think that'll take?"
"I'm an optimist. I think the whole thing is a house of cards. It could fall anytime. A currency crisis could bring it down."

"What'll happen then?"
"That depends on who the soldiers and cops side with. If it's with the people, we could have a peaceful transition. If it's with the government, it'll be bloody. We'll have helicopter gunships firing on crowds trying to take over banks and factories. It'll be Kent and Jackson State, but this time with machine guns. And the victims will be called domestic terrorists.

"I'd a lot rather that the transition be peaceful. But one way or another it has to happen.

"The war needs to come home. The violence and oppression that the USA has been supporting overseas for decades has to come back on us. Then we'll see change.

"The government's already worried about this. That's why we've got the Patriot Act — to be used against us. And that's one of the reasons for the big scare about child pornography on the Internet — to justify blocking websites and searching our computers. The other reason is to divert the grief and suppressed rage people feel at our military for killing thousands of children. The conservatives defuse that anger by channeling it onto boogie-man targets — pornographers, child molesters, abortionists.

"When Bush & Co invaded, I knew I couldn't just sign petitions and march in demonstrations anymore. That wasn't going to have any effect on these guys. I had to do what I could to keep them from waging war, to take away their equipment, to bankrupt them. The people running the show are just businessmen. If they see it's costing them more than they can get out of it, they'll stop. So I decided to start destroying expensive military items.

"I took off in a pickup truck with a camper and a dirt bike to become a domestic guerrilla. Slept in the camper so I didn't leave records at motels. Showered at truck stops. I used the bike to scout out targets and escape routes.

"I found out that security around the big bases was tight, so I started checking out National Guard branches. I liked the idea of taking revenge on the Guard for Kent State. I found a unit that had all their trucks and jeeps locked in the motor pool behind a chainlink fence, but someone had left a staff car parked behind the building. I guess the colonel didn't want to have to walk very far.

"I decided to go for it, but this first time was damn near my last. I set myself on fire. I made the mistake of starting at the top. I poured gasoline over the trunk of the car above the gas tank, and then more under the tank. But without my knowing it, the gas ran down onto the sleeve of my coat. When I flicked the lighter, my whole arm caught fire. The car did too, of course, and I had to run away from it with a blazing arm. By the time I got the coat off, I had third degree burns. Hurt like hell but I couldn't scream. Scared to.

"But it was great seeing the car go up. When the vapor in the gas tank gets hot enough, it explodes, not a huge explosion, but enough to set off the whole tank, which erupts into a fireball that swallows the car. You can feel the concussion and a blast of heat. Everything is flames. It's quite a scene, a real charge.

"Getting away, I could hardly steer the bike, my arm hurt so much. I didn't sleep that night because of the pain. Terrible oozing blisters, skin peeling off. I'd brought a first-aid kit with salve and stuff, but this was way past that.

"I was afraid to go to the emergency room because they might call the cops — a guy comes in with burns right after an arson fire. But next morning I headed for the down side of downtown.

"I had tried heroin once years ago and didn't like its down, shut-off feeling. But now I needed it. I went to the bus station, knowing that's a good place to score in most cities. I could pick up on dealer vibes, having been one myself, so I talked to this guy who was hanging out there, standing and looking around rather than just sitting and waiting for a bus. At first he was suspicious, but he sensed I wasn't a cop. A dealer has to have that instinct or he won't last long.

"I probably paid twice as much as his regular customers, but I got a balloon. Mixed a quarter spoonful with orange juice, drank it down. Bitter. I threw up and had to take some more. But a half hour later I was fine.

"I bought the newspaper and read about "Arsonist Torches National Guard" with a picture of the burned-out car. I felt great. I knew that the money it was going to take to replace that car couldn't be used to bomb Afghanistan. This had a lot more impact than writing a congressman or shouting slogans in a protest march. It made a bottom-line difference. I wanted to save the newspaper, but it could've connected me, so I threw it away.

"By then I was getting woozy. Went back to the truck and passed out. Pain woke me up in a few hours, I took some more smack and nodded out again.

"I've still got the scars, patches of turkey skin."

"That didn't make you stop?"

"No, it made me realize what all the people who've been hit by US napalm and white phosphorous are going through. Right this moment men, women, and children are crying in agony because of our bombing. And they don't have the luxury of pain killers.

"It's worse for the kids. They have a lifetime of pain ahead of them, because the scars don't grow. As the skin around them grows, that stretches the scars. The tissue becomes very thin and sensitive. It hurts for the rest of their lives.

"Hundreds of thousands of people in Vietnam and Cambodia are still living with this on a daily basis. And now Iraqi and Afghan children are facing this future.

"My pain gave me just a taste of what they are suffering. It also made me aware how terrible it would be if someone got caught in one of my fires. I'd never torch a building. Just vehicles. I even look in those to make sure no one's sleeping in the back.

"My burns made me see that what I was doing was important, trying to stop this war machine.

"If Americans knew, I mean really opened our hearts to the mass suffering we're inflicting on Iraq and Afghanistan at this moment, we'd overthrow this government. Not to mention what we did in El Salvador, Nicaragua, Chile, Indonesia, the Congo, Iran, and so many more. But we don't want to know. We turn it off — it's a long ways away. And the media sure don't want to tell us about it. Their job is to distract us from it with all sorts of nonsense.

"We close our eyes to the killing because it conflicts with the patriotic fantasies about America we learned as children. Reality is too disturbing, so we deny it. Our love of country has blinded us.

"But deep down we do know. We push it away, but it sinks into our subconscious and festers there and pops out in sick ways. That's why we have so many crazy shootings.

"We're convinced our society is good, because that's what we were taught. But good societies don't kill millions of people. Pathological ones do that. And you don't cure pathology with reforms. It needs major surgery."

"What do you see as your greatest triumph?"

"The Air National Guard watches their planes pretty carefully, but I found one parked at an unguarded airstrip. This was in the middle of the day, and I was hoping it would still be there at night. It was, and no one around. I needed more gas because the flames had to reach higher, and I wasn't sure where the tanks were. I soaked some boards with gas and laid them against the fuselage and on the wings. The plane went up fine. A beautiful sight. Had a different smell because of the aviation fuel."

"Are you going to get more planes?"

"I hope so, but the vehicles are easier to find. My favorite are the deuce-and-a-halves, those big trucks with canvas covers. They make a huge fireball, and they're expensive. That's what this game is about — make the war too expensive, so it becomes bad economics. There's lots of ways to do that, and this is my way.

"A couple of times a year, but not in any regular pattern, I take off and look for targets of opportunity. My wife keeps the home fires burning while I go out and set a fire. I follow the basic principles of guerrilla warfare — pick the time and place to attack, make it quick, and get out before the enemy can react.

"Once I almost got caught. I always pick Guard units of the edge of town, somewhat isolated. Those are less likely to be patrolled by the police, and they offer quicker access to escape routes, trails where only the bike can go. This place looked good, and they'd left a truck out. Right after it erupted in flames, though, I heard a siren and saw flashing lights. A patrol car must've been cruising nearby.

"He was between me and my escape route, so I had to take off on the bike in the other direction. He saw me, even though I was running without lights. I was hoping he'd first go to the fire, but no such luck — he charged after me. The bike is fast, but so was he. I kept turning corners because I could do that faster than he could, but he caught up on the straights. I zigzagged back onto the main road towards the escape trail, but by then other sirens were approaching from different directions.

"He was right behind me as I got to the trail. I was afraid he was going to run me over and claim it was an accident. As I slowed down to turn left onto the trail, he swung beside me into the oncoming lane and blocked me off. I couldn't turn, just had to keep going.

"Up ahead was an intersection. I raced towards it and swung a wide u-turn in the middle of it, so I could get back to the trail. But he turned his car sideways to block the road. His front tires covered the right shoulder I wanted to drive on, and I couldn't turn sharp enough to get behind him.

"I was going fast and had only a split second to react. I plunged the bike down into the drainage channel next to the shoulder of the road, right in front of his headlights. I could barely hold it stable. I skidded on the wet bottom of the channel, almost laid it down, but kicked out with my foot and managed to stay up. Then I hit an old tire and lost control. The bike bounced up and keeled over, and I scraped through the mud, wrenching my leg and banging my knee, and finally stopped, front wheel still spinning. I was hurting and covered with dreck.

"The patrol car was backing around to get me. My engine had stalled, but it started again on the first kick. I roared up the side of the channel at an angle, back onto the pavement.

"The cop was closing fast, and I moved onto the shoulder so he couldn't cut me off from the trail again. Another patrol car was speeding from town, red lights flashing, siren blaring, but he wasn't close yet. Approaching the trail, I slowed just enough to slue through the turn. As I careened down the trail away from the road, I imagined the cop swearing at me in frustration.

"I was on a tractor path leading into a big area of cornfields, and the tall corn swallowed me up in a second, friendly and protective. It was dark in there, but I kept my lights off so they wouldn't reflect off the stalks and show my position. I slowed down and laughed out loud in the warm, fragrant September night.

"The fields ran for miles, gridded with other tractor paths, and I was sure they couldn't find me here in the dark. The feed corn was so dense that even with a helicopter they'd have to be right above me before they could spot me. I was safe here until dawn.

"This was my territory now, but the streets were enemy territory, and I was going to have trouble getting out of there. When I had to try, my best bet would be a road with lots of traffic, so I could blend in. The cops couldn't be everywhere.

"A state highway ran north of town, and I headed for it, now pushing the bike so they couldn't tell my direction from its sound. It took hours. I had to cross a couple of gravel roads, first waiting out of sight until it felt safe, then running across. Finally I could hear the highway ahead. It was almost dawn, but I wanted to wait until rush-hour traffic, so I lay down and tried to sleep. The ground was cold, I was hungry, my knee hurt, and a field mouse scampered over me, but I managed to doze.

"About 7:30 I crept up towards the highway, peering out from my tractor path, afraid again. To my relief, there were enough motorcycles on the road that I figured the cops couldn't stop them all. I waited until I felt lucky, then started the bike, accelerated along the shoulder, and joined the stream between two big trucks. I saw one cop, but he was going the other way. I kept expecting a patrol car to pull beside me with a shotgun leveled out the window, but it didn't happen.

"I stopped in the next town and hid the bike near a shopping center. I was covered with mud, so I bought new clothes, cleaned up as best I could and changed, then ate a big farmer's breakfast of steak and eggs, grits, and three cups of coffee. It was the sort of place where cops might stop for doughnuts, but none came in. Poor guys must've all had to work overtime.

"I took a cab back to near where my truck was parked, drove back to the bike and loaded it in, drove a hundred more miles, and collapsed into the bunk. My body was still clogged with fear, my leg was swollen and aching, I had a nervous tic in my cheek, but I was almost glowing with bliss as I sank into sleep.

"It was a long time before I went on another sabotage mission, though.

"Once I had a close call at what looked like a perfect set-up — a jeep parked behind a Guard admin building, secluded, dark, no one around. As usual I waited an hour after the bars closed, so the streets would be emptier. Also it was a regular work night, so fewer late partygoers. But as soon as I took the lid off the gas can, this car pulls in and two guys get out, drunk. They were fumbling at their zippers to piss when they noticed me by the jeep. They shouted at me — probably thought I was trying to steal it. Seeing their chance to become heroes, they forgot about their bladders and started towards me. One of them pulled out a knife.

"Part of me wanted to throw the gas can at them and light it, but I couldn't do that. I know what burns are like. Instead I threw the can at an angle between us. The gas spewed out in a long trail, and when I lit it, the flames leaped up, high enough to reach their zippers if they'd tried to get through. That stopped their charge long enough for me to take off on the bike while they were shaking their fists and swearing at me.

"Never did get that jeep. Went back a year later and everything was locked up.

"Once I found two jeeps and a truck parked together. What a blaze they made! Someday I'm hoping to get a whole motor pool ... or a squadron of planes."

"Your work sounds pretty violent."

"It's not violent! Violence means harming people. I'm very careful not to do that.

"It's only because our culture worships property that we see destroying war machines as violence. What I'm doing is depriving the military of their tools of violence. I'm decreasing their ability to harm people. Since they refuse to disarm, I'm doing it for them.

"But I admit I've got some psychological quirks. I like fire — the huge eruption of flames is magnificent. Torching is an adrenaline high ... like dealing. Apparently I need that. Maybe that makes me neurotic, but if so, I've managed to channel my neurosis into a socially useful activity — destroying war machines. The real crazies are those who go along with this system and think they're sane.

"It's probably true that certain personality traits make people more likely to oppose their society. But conservatives use that to discount the rebels' objections by branding them abnormal. They dismiss their political views as being symptoms of psychopathology. They say radicals have emotional problems ... they're not well adjusted ... they have bad relationships with their fathers.

"But what does it mean to be well adjusted to a society like this? It means you've accepted and internalized its values. If you think about what those values really are, it's insane to do that. The people who do are normal only in the sense that they're the majority.

"And since most fathers are the spear carriers of patriarchy, since they *are* the power structure, how can we not oppose them? That kind of authority needs to be defied.

"Having a 'good' relationship with your father isn't necessarily good. It tends to make people support the powers that be, to want to please them. Kids who need their father's approval turn into toadies. That's the only way to please a patriarch. If we want to build a new kind of person, we have to become different from the old kind, and that usually means displeasing them."

"Would you prefer matriarchy?"

"I'd prefer no-archy. No group should have power over another group. That's what anarchy means.

"Conservatives conveniently forget that they're supporting this culture because of their own personality traits. And look at those — the desire to placate authority rather than defy it, to actually become the authority and have power over others, to preserve with violence if necessary an unjust economic system that denies the majority of humanity the basics of a secure life. Those are conservatives. And if you put them under pressure, they become fascists, as we're seeing."

"What amazes me, though, is how few people are seeing it. Most of them are going along with it. Young people too. They seem more interested in fitting into the system than in changing it."

"Well, most of us were too, really. As soon as the draft ended and we knew we weren't going to have to fight in Vietnam, most of our generation stopped protesting and went to work for business. The goals changed from ending war to buying a new car.

"You're right, though. A lot of the younger people coming after us became conservatives. But they grew up under a media barrage about how terrible radicals are. We were portrayed as scary, depraved freaks, like Charles Manson, who actually wasn't a radical at all, but a right-wing racist. Radicals were painted as evil villains who want to destroy everything. The political changes we want were totally ignored.

"The media also try to erase dangerous concepts from our minds by wiping out the meaning of the words. They've become our brain police. 'Radical' comes from the Latin word for 'root.' A radical is someone who wants to solve social problems by changing their root cause, instead of the liberal way of surface reforms that leave the structure the same.

"This concept of fundamental change is threatening, so the media distorted the meaning of the word 'radical' by using it for both right- and left-wingers, anyone outside the political center. They turned it into a synonym for 'extremist,' a lunatic fringer. But right-wingers can't be radical in the true sense. They're trying to preserve the root structure and roll back what changes have been made.

"The media also use ridicule to undercut dangerous ideas. A peace activist becomes a peacenik, some weirdo nut. The threat of scorn has a great effect on young people, who need to fit in, to be accepted. Being branded as a geek is death for them. They sense intuitively how status-oriented and competitive our society is, how many losers there are, and they desperately don't want to be in that group, because those are the weak people. You can finally feel strong by putting them down.

"Other words — like 'imperialism,' 'bourgeoisie,' 'system' — have important meanings, but the words have been made to seem gauche and out of style, so people are embarrassed to use them. The media pundits ridicule the words to avoid dealing with their reality. They want those concepts to fade away.

"Another successful media campaign was about changing the public perception of the Vietnam War and the US military. The movie *The Deerhunter* was crucial in this. It showed nice American prisoners of war being tortured by sadistic Vietnamese. Instead of being invaders and aggressors, Americans became the victims. By reversing the roles, the media erased My Lai from our minds.

"This perceptual switch was reinforced by the MIA movement. Tremendous press attention was given to rumors that Vietnam was still holding US prisoners. Stories of our poor soldiers languishing away in jungle prison camps were being burned into our minds decades after the war ended. Clearly Vietnam had nothing to gain by this, and no evidence for it has ever been found. But the propaganda convinced Americans that these Communists are totally vicious people."

"I agree, the ballyhoo over MIAs was a fraud. In that war there were all sorts of ways to die and never have your body found."

"I think the purpose of all the furor was to prevent any public recognition of our guilt in the killing of millions of people just because we didn't like their economic system. If we could have confronted this and accepted our responsibility and tried to change, we could've grown into a more peaceful society. But then we wouldn't want to invade other countries, and that would be threatening to the empire.

"After the war Hollywood also produced many movies designed to improve the image of the peacetime military. They showed soldiers as admirable people and military life as positive, like films of the 1950s did after the Korean War.

"So kids growing up in the '70s and '80s were subjected to a PR campaign to restore good feelings about America. And it worked. But now the image has cracked again, and people can see through it.

"We've got a whole new group of militant kids coming up. They have a deeper understanding than we did. That's partly because they learned from us, especially from our mistakes. They're not as into drugs, and they don't think they can end war just by playing the guitar.

"They're also more militant because their lives are harder than ours were. Most of them don't have the same chance to sell out that our generation did. The cushy jobs aren't there anymore, and living outside the economy has got tougher. Welfare is gone. More cops to bust you. Jail time is longer and meaner. It's a locked-down land.

“The young people who are standing up to that are a courageous bunch. My wife and I have got to know a new network of traveler kids who’ve turned against the mainstream. They stay on the move, poor as can be, most of them smart, all of them refusing to live the franchised life that surrounds them. They’re determined to ‘Live free or die.’

“Some of them do die. One girl we knew jumped bail on a bad check charge to avoid three years in prison. She was hiding out, camping, but didn’t have the right gear. She got caught in a sleet storm, chilled to the bone, everything she had soaked. When she got sick, she thought it was just a cold. When it got worse, she thought about going to the emergency room, but she heard the cops check the register there, so she decided to tough it out. She didn’t have money for a private doctor. Her temperature shot over 105, and she died of pneumonia. A bottle of IV antibiotics would’ve saved her.

“A young friend, talented musician, got busted for credit card fraud, and the judge gave him a hard nickel — five years without possibility of parole. At nineteen, five years seemed the rest of his life. He hanged himself in his cell.

“Another guy, his girl friend was pregnant, they were happy about it but had no place to raise the baby, couldn’t afford the three months upfront rent for an apartment. He got desperate, felt he had to be the male provider, so he stuck up a liquor store. Clerk shot him in the back as he was leaving with $300.

“It’s hard to survive as a young rebel these days, and I respect these kids. They’re under the hammer.

“I think with them we’re building up to another period like the ’60s, a mass outbreak of rebellious energy. And this time *we* get to be the wise elders, like Herbert Marcuse and Frantz Fanon were for us.”

“I don’t think any of our generation measure up to Marcuse and Fanon.”

“No, not as theorists. But now we don’t need more theory. What the younger generation needs is practical guidance in how to bring the system down without getting crushed in the process. And we've learned about that because we've seen how many of us did get crushed. Those of us who've stayed in the struggle and survived have a lot to teach."

"Do you have a protégé, someone to, so to speak, pass the torch on to?"
"No. This business is too risky. I'd feel terrible if something happened to them. Also there's the security issue. With all the government surveillance and infiltration, this sort of work has to be done alone. No one knows what I do except my wife, and they can't make her testify against me."

"Why tell me?"
"I know you won't turn me in. And if they waterboarded you — always a possibility these days — well, you don't know where I live or what my name is now. All you have is a webmail address.

"But it is a calculated risk. I want to go public in an anonymous way to let people know what's happening with the resistance movement. The government is hushing up about all the sabotage that's going on. It's not just me. I'm just a small part of it. There's a growing movement to undermine the machine from within. People are trashing recruiters' offices, slashing their tires, cutting their phone wires, grafittiing-out their billboards. In universities they're squirting glue into the locks of ROTC departments, stealing their mail, hacking into their computers. Autonomes are vandalizing the homes of politicians and corporate execs. The government and corporations have had to set up internal security units to catch their own people who are sabotaging them — leaking secret memos, destroying equipment, zapping computer files. A militant threw a log under the wheels of an arms train and derailed it. It's only a matter of time before a vet sets up a mortar outside an air base and starts blowing up Stealth bombers.

"The war is coming home where it belongs. But this is just starting, and the government doesn't want people to know. They're scared it'll spread."

"Do you want it to spread?"
"Yes. I'm convinced that's the only way to stop these wars. Make it too costly for the USA to extend its empire. We need to lame the beast so it can't attack anymore. We have to maximize chaos on all fronts, a thousand different kinds of uprisings so the country becomes ungovernable. That's the only way to break their hold and build something new."

"That's going to make things tougher at home."
"Yep, it will ... for a while. And that's why a lot of people are against it. They don't want to lose their comfort level. That's more important to them than the lives of millions of people overseas ... and the lives of their own grandchildren.

"You can't blame people for wanting to have a pleasant life, but in times like these, that turns them into accomplices with the system. The only way life can stay pleasant now is if you play along. The punishments for opposition are getting increasing unpleasant.

"But rebelling is invigorating. It's an authentic life, not the superficial pleasantries of a lackey life.

"Even the lackeys are going to lose their precious comfort level before long. Things are getting worse and worse here because that's the nature of the system. It devours everything.

"The country is run by corporate robots. They're squeezing the people at home and strangling them overseas. And the military is their enforcer. It's become a monster rampaging out of control, fighting enemies that it itself created, like Saddam Hussein, Osama bin Laden, the Taliban. This beast knows only to kill, and it does that reflexively, mechanically, massively. The leaders elected to stop it end up serving it. Amerika is running amok in a mania of unconscious killing. Amerika is a berserker battling the universe, a gut-shot hyena devouring its own entrails.

"We have to stop doing this ... and we can. We don't need to live this way, by bombing and killing.

"I want people to know there's a movement here to resist militarism. It's rolling. They can be part of it ... in many ways."

"Would you recommend people burn trucks?"
"I would not. It's very dangerous."

"What would you recommend that people do?"
"That's a question only they can answer."

"What if you get caught? Would you shoot it out?"
"No, I don't have any weapons. I don't believe in killing people for peace. And cops are still people.

"I'd probably spend the rest of my life as a prisoner of war in Guantánamo West, that new supermax in Colorado."

"Doesn't that scare you?"
"You bet it does. But even if that happens, my life will have meant something. I'll have done what I could to stop this monster from invading more countries and murdering more people.

"But I don't think it will happen. I'm very careful. I want to continue the struggle. As Ed Sanders said, 'Resist and Survive.'"

— 11 —

Peace Chaplain

A seminary student wrote about learning to love her enemies.

To celebrate Armed Forces Day the military base near my seminary held an open house, a public relations extravaganza to improve their image and boost recruiting. They invited the public in for a marching-band parade, a precision flying show, and a sky diving demonstration. They even offered free lemonade and cookies.

A subversive seminarian, namely me, decided to disrupt the festivities and remind people that the military's job is murder. I bought a jump suit and dyed it orange like the uniforms the prisoners in Guantánamo have to wear. I bought two U-shaped bike locks, three diapers, and a pair of old-people's rubber underpants.

All suited up, I had a friend drive me onto the base before people started arriving for the celebration. She dropped me off at the traffic circle just inside the main gate, kissed me on the cheek for good luck, and drove back out the gate. In the center of the traffic circle stood a flagpole flying the Stars and Stripes. I ran to the pole, fastened my foot to it with one bike lock and my neck to it with the other — pretty uncomfortable — and started shouting, "Close Guantánamo! No More Abu Ghraibs! Free the Prisoners!" People gawked as they drove by, some laughing like I was part of the show, some waving, some giving me the finger.

I had an anti-war speech all prepared to give the reporters. I had a bottle of water in one pocket and a bag of trail mix in the other and was wearing the diapers and rubber underpants for toilet emergencies. I was locked on for a long stay.

A couple of minutes later, a van and a truck full of soldiers drove up. The GIs jumped out and surrounded me. They stood at attention facing the traffic, blocking me off from view. The van backed in next to me. I shouted my slogans louder, and they started singing "The Star-Spangled Banner" to drown me out. To people driving in, it must've looked like a patriotic demonstration — soldiers around the flag singing to greet them.

A GI grabbed me from behind. Another wrapped duct tape around my mouth, then continued around my head to cover my eyes, leaving only a little space at the nose for breathing. I thrashed my arms in panic, but they pinned them behind my back, almost strangling me in the process, and taped my wrists together. Helpless and terrified, I got a tiny hint of what life must be like for the prisoners. Nobody said a word to me; the only sound was the national anthem.

One of them jerked the lock that was around my neck, twisting the metal against my throat. I heard the sound of aerosol spray and smelled fumes. They're gassing me, I thought. The metal on my neck got very cold. The bang of a hammer on the lock against the pole sent a shock through me, flashing pain down my spine and up to my inner ears and eyes. Three hammer blows and the lock fell off. They must've frozen it with the spray to make it brittle enough to break. Then they broke the lock on my leg and taped my ankles together.

Before today, I'd had a condescending attitude towards soldiers and was fond of quoting, "Military intelligence is an oxymoron." But I had to admit this was a brilliant counterattack. It was so well prepared, as if they'd been expecting something like this. I had told some fellow students about my plan, and one of them might've tipped off the military. I hate to think that, but it could be. We're living more and more in a society of informers, a proto-police state where the government encourages its citizens to report their neighbors for disloyal activities.

Two GIs picked me up, heaved me into the back of the van, slammed the door, and drove away. Now I got really scared. Where were they taking me? What were they going to do to me? I tried to pray, but my mind was screaming too loud.

After about twenty minutes they stopped. I could hear them whispering in the front seat. They seemed to be arguing — maybe about whether to kill me after they raped me. I'd read if you're about to be raped and you shit your pants, it's good protection — you make yourself too repulsive. I tried but couldn't.

They opened the door, pulled me out, and dropped me on the ground. I heard them unzipping their pants.

Then I felt a stream of warm liquid on my face. I turned away but caught another stream from the other side. They peed all over me, laughing but still not saying anything. Then they kicked dirt on me like a dog would do and drove away.

Maybe it's over, I thought, maybe that was it. I'd never felt worse in my life, totally fouled and degraded. Rage rose in me and turned to nausea; as I vomited, my breakfast came out my nose but clogged there against the tape, almost suffocating me. Finally I blew enough out so I could breathe. My stomach kept spasming; I was quivering all over; my throat and nose burned from acid.

I kept telling myself it could've been worse. Although I was relieved that all they'd done was relieve themselves on me, I still loathed them. I was pretty sure what they did wasn't part of the official plan, but a bit of individual initiative.

I tried to pull my hands and feet from the tape but couldn't. I tried to stand up but fell back down. Giving up, I cried and cried, and the tears welled against the tape. Finally I stopped trying anything and just lay there, empty of tears ... of hope ... of thoughts. A wave of pain rolled through me, then out. The havoc of my mind stilled. In the quiet came a yearning for God stronger than anything I'd known before. My whole being reached out for the Lord.

A name rose from deep within me, and I called it out into the silence: *Jesus*. The name struck the hollow bell of my emptiness and reverberated through me, shimmering, fading, sounding again: *Jesus*. As the name pulsed within, a wash of comfort flowed over me. Like the balm of Gilead,[7] it suffused inside, calming and steadying me. The presence of Christ increased, becoming a flow of love that encompassed me. My fear vanished, and in its place came a voice:

Do you want out of this hell?
Yes!

Do you know the way out?
No.

Love is the way. You have to love even your enemies.
Oh ... that sounds familiar.

Yes, I've said it before. But sometimes we need to be reminded.
Those guys who just peed on me ... I'm supposed to love them.

I never said it was easy ... but that's the way out.
Can You help me love them?

Certainly. You need to understand that their own suffering made them do it. They have so much pain inside, and they think they can get rid of it by pushing it onto someone else. Of course that doesn't work, but it's all they know.
Thank you. I can see how that's true, and I'll work on really understanding it. Then what do I do?

Then you have to forgive them.
I'll try.

Remember I once said: "Forgive them, Father, for they know not what they do." I still have to say that. Every day. They're

7 Several Bible verses refer to Gilead as the source of healing balm. In all likelihood this ancient trade item was what is now known as balsam of Mecca, the resinous gum of a tree native to southern Arabia.

not really your enemies. They're just hurt human beings. Like me.

Like you and everybody else. That's why I'm here.
I could feel my suffering covering me, but now it was transparent and I could see through it to those two soldiers and sense their suffering too. Theirs was just like mine. My arrogance towards them had the same roots as their aggression towards me. I thought about how they'd probably grown up, all the garbage that had been poured into them by the society and their pain-filled parents. Now they are trapped in fear and self-hatred. When they project that onto someone else and attack her, they feel better for a little while. But then it creeps back over them, worse now.

You're starting to understand. Sometimes great pain can help us see. By hurting you, the men locked themselves deeper into their own prisons, into hell. That's what sin is.
In my mind I held the image of two GIs I'd never seen and tried to love them. It was hard. I kept hoping Jesus would say something so I could stop. But He didn't. I had to bring love up within me and send it out to them. As I kept trying, I could feel the love of Christ flowing into me, filling me until I was brimming, and then overflowing out to them. It was all the same love, just like it was all the same pain. Now the guys looked different, like two hurt children. Children of God.

If they hadn't done that awful thing to you, you wouldn't have learned this, and this is more important.
Now I see You're right. I can always take a shower, but what You showed me will stay with me. Thank you, Lord.

Thank them, too.
Even that? Oh no, it's really not easy, is it?

No, but it's worth it.
As I tried to be grateful to the guys for this lesson, gradually I felt an attitude of gratitude, not just to them but to

everything that had happened to me in life because it had all brought me to where I was now, having my first deep communication with Christ. Definitely worth it. Suddenly happy, I laughed into my duct-tape gag.

Now you've got it. Now you're ready to free yourself. You can do it.

I moved my hands back and forth, twisting them against the tape. Before, I had tried with sudden jerks, but now I worked slowly, tugging with one hand and then the other. Gradually the tape gave way, and I was able to pull one hand out. I raised it in the air like a wonder, full of the power of gentleness. The twisting had broken my watchband, though. I freed the other hand from its sticky manacle, then peeled the tape from my head, tearing out clumps of hair as I went, blinking into the sudden light, gulping fresh air.

I was near a dirt road surrounded by brush and trees. Wet, sticky and stinky, I unfettered my feet, stood up, shook my arms and legs to make sure they still worked, and shouted in rage and joy. I'd worn a T-shirt and shorts under the jump suit, so I pulled the filthy thing off and threw it into the bushes.

Jesus, I prayed, You were there all the time, but now I know You better. We're a team. And I'll keep trying to love the people life sends me.

I walked down the road, hoping it was in the right direction. But loving people doesn't mean letting them abuse me. I didn't want these guys to think what they'd done was OK. Then they'd keep doing it.

I considered going to the police. Although I'd never seen their faces, the urine would have their DNA. But how to find them? There were thousands of GIs on the base, and I doubted that the military would be cooperative. Plus if I filed a complaint, my name would go on an official list. As it was now, I didn't know who they were, but they didn't know who I was either, and that would help with a plan that was forming in my mind.

I needed to learn to love all soldiers, to stop thinking of them as enemies and see their divine nature, to realize they do what they do because of their own suffering. If I didn't have any more contact with them, I'd probably slip back into my old attitudes. But if I was a military chaplain and pastored them, I'd be continually reminded of their true worth. I could actively love them.

You can love people and still oppose their behavior. Jesus loved the money-changers while He was driving them from the temple. A parent loves a child but still has to punish sometimes.

Soldiers are worthy of love, but to really love a violent person means trying to change them, to keep them from harming others and thereby themselves, to save them from their own ignorant acts. Love carries obligation.

As I walked home, I decided to become a chaplain after I'm ordained and work for change. But not in the nice liberal sense of joining the system and trying to make it a little more humane here and there. That ameliorative approach is an appealing idea, but it hasn't worked. It just strengthens the structure by making it function better and reducing the pressure for transformation. I think at this point we need to break the military, the government and the corporations, not improve them.

I know this sounds severe, but if we read US and British history without nationalistic blinders, it's obvious we're continually intruding in other countries to further our own economic interests. American-British foreign policy is an ongoing crime against humanity. At home this is concealed with altruistic rhetoric about saving the world from vile foes, but in the target countries, our aggression and its purposes are very clear. People there are now responding with what we label terrorism, but actually we are the top terrorist armed to the teeth with weapons of mass destruction. The alliance of US and British elites threatens the rest of the world in a whole spectrum of ways.

During World War One, the British persuaded the Arabs to fight on their side by promising them independence. Thousands of Arabs died in battle for the Brits because of this promise of freedom. But after the victory, Britain refused them independence. Instead they installed puppet kings — Faisal in Iraq and Ibn Saud in Saudi Arabia — to rule in their interest.

After World War Two, Britain and the USA pressured the United Nations into confiscating Arab land to form the state of Israel, making the Arabs pay for the crimes of the Germans. In addition to providing a nation for the Jews, Israel would be a forward base for Western economic and military power in the Mideast.

In the early 1950s, the USA and Britain overthrew the government of Iran because it tried to nationalize its oil industry, which was under Western control. We installed the Shah as dictator, and he promptly gave the oil back to us. Then he began a twenty-five year reign of terror against his own people. His secret police jailed, tortured or killed hundreds of thousands of Iranians who opposed him. Since they knew he was kept in power only by American military aid, they began hating the USA. They finally ousted the Shah, but then the CIA started subverting the new government, trying to bring it down. At that point, the Iranians fought back by holding US Embassy officials hostage, which was a mild response, considering what we had done to their country.

In the mid 1950s, Egypt decided to nationalize the Suez Canal and use the income from it to help their people out of poverty. They were willing to pay its British and French owners the full market value for their shares, but Western governments and Israel responded violently, invading and bombing Egypt into submission.

Countries have the right to nationalize their resources as long as they pay a fair compensation, so what Iran and Egypt did was legal. The Western response, though, was illegal aggression in violation of international law and the United Nations charter. It roused in its victims a deep resolve for revenge.

The USA and Britain committed similar atrocities in Iraq, Syria, Lebanon, Libya, Indonesia, and Afghanistan, all years before Muslims turned to terrorism to finally drive us out of their part of the world.

No wonder they hate us. Imagine how we would feel if a foreign country were doing this to us. We'd be fighting back any way we could.

Patriots don't like to be reminded of this history. They claim that any country that had our power would do the same, so it's better we do it than the other ones. But that's moral blindness.

The present and historical fact is that the Anglo-Saxon varieties of imperialism and capitalism are particularly harsh, exploitive and expansionist. They need to be stopped.

This view offends many Americans because we're raised to link our country and God. America is God's country, so naturally He's a patriot. And a patriarch. We're taught this theology in Sunday school, and it stays with us.

Once we overcome our conditioning, we can see that our military exists to defend a cruel economic order with strategies of mass murder. The chaplain's job is to soothe the consciences of the soldiers so they keep doing their job. That might be a fine way for some chaplains to show their love for them, but it wouldn't be right for me. I want to wake up their consciences, to make them see what they're doing and help them quit. I want to bore from within, find soldiers who are discontent and convince them to resist violence.

Of course that will bring down the wrath of the commanders. They may even send me to jail, but that would provide a public platform for exposing the viciousness of the military. Lots of Christians, from St. Paul to Martin Luther King, have gone to jail for their beliefs. I'm not in their league, but I'll serve in the way I can.

— 12 —

Refusal

A Buddhist friend of mine put me in touch with a young novice who contributed this account, which we then revised together.

Back in high school I'd been good at languages but couldn't afford to go to college, so I joined the Navy for the language training. They have a program where if you pass an aptitude test, they'll send you to the Defense Language Institute in Monterey, California, for an intensive course that's worth almost a year of college credit. Plus they have an active-duty education program that offers college courses. I figured after my discharge I could finish my education on the GI Bill, and with my language skills, I could get a job in international business.

The other military branches offer programs like this too, but the Navy seemed the best way to stay out of the fighting. I was hoping for a major language like Chinese, Russian, or Spanish, but they assigned me to Pashto, which is spoken in Afghanistan and Pakistan. After training, I'd be stationed on a ship in the Arabian Sea monitoring phone calls and radio broadcasts, listening for key words that might give a clue about where the Taliban were so the planes from the aircraft carriers could bomb them. I didn't think about this last part, though. I was focused on my future.

The study itself was a real grind — drills, exercises, and vocabulary all day long and a couple of hours at night. But no classes on weekends, so we could take off.

I couldn't afford weekends in San Francisco, but in a bookstore in Monterey I saw a poster for a two-day retreat at a Zen Buddhist center nearby. It sounded weird enough to be a good break from the military, and the price was right, so I signed up for the first of a two-weekend introductory course.

The place was beautiful, deep in the mountains and forest. The course was called Buddha Breath, Buddha Mind and was led by a bald-headed woman. Instead of an orange robe she wore blue jeans and a sweatshirt. She said first we were going to learn how to breathe. I thought, What have I got myself into?

We spent an hour just breathing in and out, and you know, it turned out to be pretty interesting. When thoughts came up, we were supposed to just nod to them, then let them go and return to our breathing. Thoughts and breathing, thoughts and breathing, and then as I kept doing this, I noticed something more, some part of me that I hadn't known before, that was watching all this going on, a quiet, wise old part who was just looking at it all and nodding OK. He'd been doing that all along without my knowing it. I thought of him as an old guy with a white beard. But he was me, that was my Buddha mind.

The next hour we were supposed to keep breathing and watching our thoughts, but at the same time notice everything happening around us right here and now. That turned out to be quite a lot. It's amazing what all is going on that we don't pay attention to because we're shut off in our thoughts — worrying about what happened in the past and what might happen in the future. Esther, the group leader, called this our monkey mind because it's always jumping from one thing to another. It gets lost in each thing and doesn't have any perspective on itself. But the Buddha mind, that silent witness, can give us a peaceful perspective on ourselves and the world.

From that deeper level I noticed how much beauty shone in simple things: a beaded curtain of eucalyptus buds swaying in the breeze, dust drifting through sunlight, a fly walking on the wall. Watching these while quietly breathing in and out, I could tell the buds, the dust, the fly, and I were all part of the Buddha mind. It wasn't just my mind but something we shared. This was a bit spooky because it meant there was more to me than me, or there was less of me than me, depending on how I looked at it.

Esther said each of us isn't an autonomous monad but an aspect of a larger wholeness. She compared the Buddha mind to the entire light spectrum, which is mostly invisible to us, and individuals to the colors we see. Colors and individuals appear to be different, but they're just sections of the overall spectrum. Continuity is more basic than differences, but we don't see it that way. The same analogy works with the ocean. We are waves that think of ourselves as self-contained units, but we're really just water that has temporarily taken on this form. Our true identity, the water, isn't born and doesn't die. It just is. The wave suffers because of its delusion of individuality, the water doesn't. This principle simultaneously destroys our concept of ourselves and gives us a greater one.

What she was saying was heavy-duty stuff, but it clicked in me because it described how I was feeling just sitting there breathing and paying attention. I signed up for the next weekend.

During the week I practiced mindful breathing and awareness as much as I could, which wasn't very much. It was almost impossible while I was listening to Pashto in the language lab. I could sort of do it during the regular classes between having to give answers. I could do it best when I was alone, but I was hardly ever alone. We did everything as a group. At meals people wanted to talk, and if I would've told them I just wanted to pay attention to my breathing, they would've thought I was crazy. Finally I came up with the trick of putting my MP3 in my ears but with no music. During meals I could eat in silence, and no one bothered me because they thought I was listening to rock songs and *that* they could understand. Some of the people I usually ate with did think I was being unfriendly, but I didn't know how to explain it.

One night as I was doing mindful breathing trying to go to sleep, all these scenes of war came rushing out at me

— people getting blown up, crippled orphans, survivors filled with a grief that turns into hatred. They took me over like an invading army. My throat tightened, and I started to hyperventilate — gasping for air, feeling like I was suffocating. Not exactly the desired effect! I kept with the mindful breathing, though, and rode the turbulence through into calmness again. Gradually I stopped trembling, and the thoughts backed off, but I knew the war was still out there waiting for me.

The second weekend was called Buddha Heart, Buddha Hands. We did walking meditations where we integrated our breath with our steps, walking slowly and noticing everything happening in and around us from the deep inner peace of mindfulness. Now we did more than observe it. We tuned in to the feeling level of what was going on. Esther told us first to feel our own emotions as we were walking, to open up to them, accept them, and embrace them with compassion. When we can accept our pain without resentment, we're ready to love our whole self, warts and all.

Sad feelings came up in me, as if they'd been waiting for this invitation. Rather than just nod to them, I asked them what the trouble was. They started complaining about all sorts of things from long ago, or they were afraid of things that maybe might happen. I felt like a parent listening to a child tell its problems, but my parents had never listened to me like that, and I'd never listened to myself either. I was in a lot more pain than I'd wanted to admit, and I just walked along feeling sorry for myself for a while. But the more I listened to the pain, the quieter it got until it sort of talked itself out, and in the silence I could feel compassion without really feeling sorry for myself. I just accepted what was there without judging it. This was the way it was. This was me.

We expanded this technique to the people around us. In sitting meditation we held the image of each of us in our minds and tried to feel what the other was feeling and to embrace that with love. Then we did this with all of humanity, practiced being aware of their pain, accepting them and loving them.

In walking meditation we applied this to all creatures and the environment they exist in. We felt the suffering of the spider starving because no one comes to its web. We felt the suffering of the fly caught in the web of another spider. None of us is separate, Esther reminded us, we are all held together in a web of suffering and love. The differences between us are a surface illusion.

As I was walking, I gazed out at the Ventana Mountains — they reminded me of home in West Virginia. Then they looked like Afghanistan. I realized West Virginia was the same as Afghanistan. Lots of suffering in both places — people caught in hardscrabble poverty, intolerant religion, rigid family roles, creating more suffering because they don't know any other way. My family and the Taliban — the same. I started to cry because I was training to help bomb my kinfolks.

In the Buddha Hands sessions Esther talked about acting on these principles to change the world and reduce suffering. She described Buddhist projects to help battered women defend themselves and forgive their attackers, to help prisoners find inner freedom, to help former child soldiers rediscover their childhood and heal their trauma. She played a video about Thich Nhat Hanh, the Vietnamese Buddhist monk who opposed the violence of both the Communists and the anti-Communists and was therefore persecuted by both sides. Suffering is caused by ignorance of our true nature, he explained, and violence is acting out that suffering onto others. We need to both overcome the ignorance with mindfulness and to end the violence with social action.

During the week I had a hard time back in the Navy. I could see I'd been deluding myself by thinking I'd be away from the fighting if I was sitting on a boat out in the ocean. I'd be an assistant killer, an accomplice to murder. I thought about the bombs being dropped right now, people blown apart, families destroyed. And for what? Because our government didn't like their government. It was obvious to me now that the whole thing was insane, and I couldn't do it. No way could I spy on people's phone and radio conversations and send a jet to kill them and anyone else who happened to be around. It wasn't just that I didn't want to; it wasn't possible. They were all me. I couldn't even be in the Navy anymore because killing was the purpose of the whole show. But the certainty of this decision scared me. The military is kind of like the Mafia — you can't just quit. They come after you.

Needing time and a clear head to figure out what to do, I cut classes (a crime in itself) and did a walking meditation on the beach. I took off my shoes to connect to the earth and water. Thoughts are like shoes: They're useful in certain situations but cut us off from contact with the deeper dimension, so I tried to get rid of them too. Our senses isolate us in our egos, so I closed my eyes and walked blind. As long as I walked from my Buddha mind, I knew where to step. I just had to trust that. It was a good exercise in living in the moment. I got my pant legs soaked and stumbled over some driftwood, but I belonged to it all. I wasn't afraid and alone anymore. Selfless, I had the strength of the universe and was filled with a calm determination to refuse to obey military orders. I knew that would mean prison, but I would treat that as a stay in a monastery and would practice mindfulness through it all. With this decision came a rush of freedom.

That evening I told some of my classmates what I was planning, in hopes a few of them might join me. If several of us refused to obey orders, that would have a lot more effect than just one person. One they can just shove away in prison and write off as a fluke. But a group would get press coverage, and we'd have a chance to explain why we were doing this. It would encourage other people, and the discontent would spread. I'd read about the Presidio 27 mutiny during the Vietnam War, how that helped turn the country against the war. When they refused to obey orders, the Army threatened to execute them all, but because of public pressure it released them after a year-and-a-half in prison, and they came out as anti-war heroes.

But instead of solidarity, I ran into solid hostility. The group turned against me. Some of them said I was on the side of Osama bin Laden, others that I was making all of them look bad.

I was disappointed but said, "If that's the way you feel, forget I mentioned it." But they didn't forget it. That night they gave me a blanket party.

I woke up to a towel being crammed into my mouth. I tried to scream, but I was gagged. Someone punched me in the stomach. I tried to get away, but I was held tight by a blanket pulled around me. They pounded me with all their might, working from the chest to the knees with particular preference for the groin. They didn't say anything so I couldn't tell who it was. They just hit. Hard.

Finally they stopped. I was crying and shaking; I hurt all over, not just from the beating but from who it was that did it. These were my mates. We'd been through a lot together. I'd thought we were friends.

I tried to come back to my breathing. Although each breath hurt, I managed to calm myself. The pain was still there, but now I had some distance from it.

I could see that the guys probably thought I'd betrayed our friendship too — one of their mates turned traitor on them, made them feel immoral for being in the military. Seeing it from the point of view of their pain helped me get back to mindfulness. This was just another example, like war, of people acting out their suffering by inflicting it on others. I could feel these guys' pain at being working-class dorks, Bush's pain at being a rich loser, the Taliban's pain at their helplessness to stop the world from changing.

Through my own pain I could feel the huge mass of collective pain that explodes into wars which then generate more pain, infecting more people with hatred. I could see that violence reproduces itself like a virus, and the way to stop it is to relieve suffering wherever we find it so it doesn't build up.

I thought about military prison and the suffering that awaited me there. I wouldn't be locked up with pacifists but with regular criminals who could be a lot meaner than the guys tonight. I might get beat up, humiliated, raped.

A few hours ago during walking meditation, going to prison to uphold my principles seemed noble. Now lying here trembling in pain it seemed nutty. I didn't need any more suffering. Been there. Done that. Got the T-shirt.

I was going to do more than just refuse to obey orders; I was refusing to go to prison too. I was deserting. Right now.

Aching all over, I tossed my few civilian things into my bag, hobbled out of the barracks, drove off the base, and spent the night in a motel outside Monterey. In the morning my body was bruised, swollen, stiff and sore, and my piss was pink, but my mind was clear and free. As soon as I thought about the future, though, I got scared. Now I was a fugitive.

I soaked in a hot bath, then meditated to bring the mind back to right now, where all the problems seemed manageable. For the first time since joining the military, I felt like a warrior, but a different kind — for peace.

I drove to the Zen center and told them what happened. They said they'd help, but we agreed I shouldn't stay there because I'd mentioned the place to a couple of the guys. Esther called around to other centers and found one where I could stay. Their roof needed mending, and I could earn my room and board that way.

I bowed to Esther in thanks, and she bowed back to me. She'd taught me an amazing amount in two weeks, really changed my life.

I sold my car so it couldn't be traced and took a long bus ride with lots of other poor people. Looking around at them, I knew that some of the younger ones were probably thinking of joining the military. They'd still be poor, but at least they'd have something. In exchange for a bit of security, they'd help their government kill people. That was their best chance in life. What does that say about our society?

Working on the roof at my new Buddhist center was a great way to experience the interconnectedness of all life. Up there in silence, I could feel how the sun was becoming part of me. It was also giving life to the plants in the garden that would then give life to us, and later our bodies when buried would give life to other plants. I thought about how the atoms of my body had been formed in the core of other suns. The people downstairs were cooking food for me while I was keeping them dry. I thought about my family and the people who would come after me, and I knew we were all more closely tied together than I'd ever imagined. At the most basic level we weren't separate, we were all just cells in this great body of God called the universe. That body was held together by the laws of physics but also by laws of love and compassion, the need to treat each other kindly and not generate more suffering. Once we see the interconnections, killing anything becomes suicide.

That made me think about how our economic system is based on ignoring these connections. People are deluded that they are separate, and that makes them so insecure and frightened that they have to grab everything they can to defend themselves, build walls of property they can hide behind, then armies to guard the walls.

I could see all that from up on the roof as I was nailing shingles mindfully, breathing mindfully, and occasionally screaming mindfully when I banged my thumb with the hammer. After finishing the roof, I worked in the garden, where it became even clearer that the plants and bugs and dirt and I are just the same divine energy temporarily expressing itself in different forms, all of it sacred and fragile and worthy of care.

I've been here a year now. Eight of us are working on staff, and many more come for courses. We do sitting and walking meditations together and try to live in each moment because that's all anyone has, but that's enough since each moment is eternity. At night we read and discuss the scriptures with our two monks, chant the Pali suttas, and go to bed early.

One of the monks is from Japan, and he's teaching me Japanese. It's a beautiful language.

— 13 —

SAMs for Uncle Sam

Merna al-Marjan is a young Iraqi who is in Germany studying European history. We talked in her dormitory room, a Spartan but functional cubicle in a building that embodies a hopeful change in European history: It was constructed in the nineteenth century as an army barracks but now houses university students. That's progress.

On Merna's small table sat a pot of peppermint tea and a plate of baklava. She's short and plump with smooth skin the color of clover honey and deep anthracite eyes; she was wearing a long skirt of light cotton, a long-sleeved blouse, and a green paisley headscarf. Though she has some English, Merna and I spoke in German. We later reworked the interview together from my English translation.

Hathaway: *"Headscarves have become a controversial item of clothing here in Germany."*

Al-Marjan: "Yes, you can't teach in the schools if you wear one. It's OK for a teacher to wear a Christian crucifix, but not a Muslim headscarf. I didn't wear a *hijab* in Iraq, but I've started doing it here to show solidarity. It's ridiculous to ban an article of clothing, a simple piece of cloth. What sort of freedom is that?

"The West has such a distorted view of Arab women. Well, of men too, but since I'm a woman, I notice that more.

"What really makes me mad is when Westerners use the way women live in the Muslim world as a justification for invading it — either with their armies or their ideas. They're convinced we should be like them. If they were happy, that would be one thing. They could say, 'Here, follow our example.' But they're much unhappier than most of us are. Their marriages and families fall apart, their children commit terrible crimes, commit suicide. Their society is fragmented into these isolated individuals who have to compete against one another. It's a wreck, but they're trying to force it onto us.

"Western women are convinced they need a career to be fulfilled, as if that's some magic thing, much better than being just a mother. But if you look at the things people actually do in their careers, most of them aren't very fulfilling. The work gets routine, then boring. I may get to be a professor, but I've been around enough of them to know that's no big deal. They just juggle ideas in the air. What people do in their jobs is trivial compared to raising a family.

"The work of being a mother is devalued here, but to be the emotional center of a family, to keep everyone in balance, to know what they need on so many different levels and to give them some of that, well, that requires a much subtler intelligence than business does. It's a deep knowledge of human beings, far more important than a job. Mothers are the real CEOs of civilization, and we need to give that power back to them, including the power to have a career, if that's what they want.

"A family needs money, but the getting of it is dominating our lives. People are either unemployed and terribly poor or they have a job and are totally exhausted. But if we took the work that needs to be done and spread it around so everyone could work a few hours a day, then we'd have time for our families and also make some money. Life would be more balanced. Some people might end up less rich, but they'd enjoy life more. They think they need so much now only because their jobs have fixated them on that. Money has become a substitute for life. There's never enough of it, because the things it can buy aren't really satisfying. They just distract us from the emptiness of our lives spent chasing money. We've become shrunken down to coins."

"It's unusual to hear a young person say things like this. Where did you learn this?"
"From my mother, of course, from talking to her and watching her. Women in my country, and probably most non-western women, understand this.

"That doesn't mean we're content with our situation. We want to change it, but by strengthening the family. Family should be the power center of the society, rather than business. In the West, home life is subservient to the outer world of work, but that's destructive. Work should serve the needs of the family, not the other way around.

"We definitely have to change the power between men and women. It has to be more equal. We need to make sure men don't harm women. But we don't need help from the all-wise Westerners to do that. Their model doesn't work even for them, so it sure won't work for us."

"How did you come to be studying in Germany?"
"I won a scholarship with an essay I wrote comparing King Faisal I and Marshal Pétain. Both of them came to power by serving imperialist conquerors. Faisal helped the British take over Iraq, and Pétain helped the Germans rule France. Both were hated by their people as traitors. The current puppet president of Iraq — he's not worth naming — is playing the same role for the Americans. But I didn't mention this last part in my essay."

"Why not?"
"Because I wanted to win the scholarship. The Germans don't mind if you criticize them, but they're very nervous about offending the Americans. They're still an occupied country. Plus they're not about to give a scholarship to someone they think might be a 'Muslim extremist.'"

"Are you a Muslim extremist?"
"No, but that doesn't matter. The Germans are running on fear now. They try to pretend they're independent of the Americans, but they're helping them in all sorts of ways to kill Iraqis and Afghans. And they know that's going to lead to revenge attacks

in their country, so they're wary now about letting Muslims into Germany. To them, we're all potential terrorists."

"How is Germany helping the USA in the war?"
"One example came out in the news recently, although it happened before the war started. Back then the Germans had spies in the Iraqi Defense Ministry, and they managed to steal a copy of the plans for defending against the US invasion — where our troops were going to be stationed, where anti-aircraft batteries would be placed, where supplies would be stored. The Germans gave those plans to the Americans, so they knew exactly where to bomb. That caused the death of tens of thousands of our soldiers. Now their families need to avenge them.

"The Germans are also helping train this new army and police in suppressing the people. And they're sending military equipment to fight the insurgency. Iraqis are being killed with weapons made in Germany. German politicians call that peace keeping, but it's actually war making. We don't forget things like that."

"Do you know people in the insurgency?"
"Of course ... some of them very well. In the West all resistance fighters are portrayed as fanatics, but many of them aren't even religious. They just want to throw the invaders out.

"Even fanatics like al-Qaeda aren't really aggressors. They're fighting a defensive war. Have you read al-Qaeda's demands?"

"No."
"I'm not surprised. The Western media never publish them because the demands are so reasonable. They basically come down to, 'Go home and leave us alone. Pull your soldiers, your CIA agents, your missionaries, your corporations out of Muslim territory. If you do that, we'll stop attacking you.' Nothing about destroying the West or forcing it to become Islamic. Just that the West should stay in the West.

"If people knew this — knew how easy it would be to stop terrorism — they wouldn't want to fight this crazy war. That's why the media ignore al-Qaeda's demands. Western leaders don't want people to see that the war's real purpose isn't to stop terrorism but to control this part of the world — my home. They actually *want* the terrorism because that gives them the excuse they need — the threat of an evil enemy."

"But how about Israel? Is that Muslim territory?"
"It's been Muslim since the time of the Prophet and continues to be, despite invasions by the Crusaders, the colonialists, and now the Zionists and Americans. We drove out the first two, and we'll drive out the second two. None of them have the right to take what belongs to the Arab people. The barbarians keep descending on us from the north, and we keep throwing them out. It's an old story.

"Just because the ancestors of the Jews might have lived there two thousand years ago doesn't give them any claim to that land today. It's absurd for them to say it belongs to them after all this time. We're not going to let them get away with it."

"Would you consider yourself a resistance fighter?"
"To the extent that one can fight with ideas, yes. I don't believe in setting bombs, though. But my brother does. He didn't start out that way, though. He used to be pro-American. He got his PhD in physics there. He likes the people and still has friends there. But he's come to hate the government."

"What happened to him?"
"Well ... it happened to our whole family."

"Tell me about it."
Merna glanced away, grimaced, and chewed on her cheek for a moment. "One night very late I woke up to a huge crash. The house was shaking. I thought it was an earthquake, then I thought it was a bomb. I heard shouts downstairs.

Someone was in our home. All I could think was, 'They'll kill us! I don't want to die in my pajamas.'

"Then I thought, 'Better in pajamas than naked.' I was afraid whoever it was would rape me and then kill me. I wanted to jump out the window, but it was the second floor and I was too afraid. Then I thought, 'Jumping is my only chance. If I don't break my leg, maybe I can run away. Where, though? Anywhere, just away.'

"I put on a robe and shoes and went to the window. Men with guns were standing in our yard, soldiers with little American flags sewn on their sleeves. Their truck was parked in front of our house. I couldn't run away.

"Inside the house men were stamping up our stairs, shouting something I didn't understand. One of them kicked my door open, and another one shined a flashlight on me. The flashlight was on his rifle, which was pointed at me. I screamed and prayed, *'Allahu Akbar.'*

"The door kicker ran at me, grabbed my hand, and dragged me downstairs. I fell onto the stairs, but he just kept dragging. My father, mother and brother were in the living room, all of them in pajamas. My mother was shaking and crying. The door to our house wasn't there anymore. They'd blown it off. The air was smoky.

"While two soldiers pointed their rifles at us, the others searched us. They made us raise our arms and spread our legs, then they patted all over our bodies. One of them stuck his hand between my legs and smirked. Another squeezed my mother's breasts.

"My brother shouted and lunged at the man, but the Americans grabbed him. I heard a shot — so close it hurt my ears — and thought they'd killed him, but then pieces of the ceiling fell down — one of them had shot into the air. They pushed my brother to the floor and kicked him in the head and stomach and between his legs. He tried to kick back until one of them put the barrel of his gun to his head. My brother stopped, and they punched him in the face, yanked his arms behind his back, snapped handcuffs on him, and kicked him again, calling him a 'sand nigger.' Then they handcuffed my father to keep him from defending us.

"'Now they're going to rape mom and me and make my father and brother watch, then kill us all,' I thought.

"My father is a gentle man. He's a professor of Arabic literature, retired now. Seeing him so helpless and humiliated ... it broke my heart. And I'd never seen hatred on his face until that moment.

"After they searched us, they demanded to see our identity papers. Imagine — they break into our house and demand to see our identity papers, as if we don't belong here. When we gave them the papers, they compared our names to a list they had. 'Where is Ahmad al-Marjan?' one of them shouted at us. 'I am Ahmed al-Marjan. I don't know any Ahmad,' my father answered. 'You've got the same last name, you must know him. Where is he?' the American demanded. 'There are thousands of al-Marjans. I do not know them all. You have the wrong house. You have attacked the wrong family. You have ruined our home for nothing,' my father said.

"In fact Ahmad was our cousin, and he was in the resistance. We knew where his parents lived, but he'd gone underground, sleeping in different houses, striking at the Americans and their puppet police whenever he could find the opportunity. I was terrified the Americans would torture us into giving information on him. How much did they already know? If they knew he was our cousin, then they would know we were lying to them, and they would torture us more. What would the torture be? Whatever it was, I didn't think I could take it. But if I told about him, and they arrested him or killed him, how could I live with myself? I'm sure our whole family was having similar thoughts.

"'Are any of you in the resistance?' the American demanded. "No,' my father answered. 'Who do you know in the resistance?' 'No one that I know of. People do not tell such things.' 'Do you have any weapons or explosives or information about the resistance?' 'No.' 'If you have any, and you tell us now, we'll let you go. But if you say no and we find it, we'll take you to prison.' 'We have nothing.'

"They made us lie on the floor, then searched the house — dumping out drawers, knocking books off shelves. They pulled up the rug, I guess to see if we had a trap door, turned over furniture and cut open the cushions on the divan. All the while one of them was pointing his rifle at us.

"These men stank. Their bodies were dirty, their clothes were dirty. They were disgusting. Muslims are very clean people, and it was an insult just to have these filthy soldiers in our home, let alone that they were destroying it. You could tell they were afraid, but they covered it up by being mean. They threw cigarette butts on our rug and smeared them out with their boots. They spat on the floor.

"Some of them went into my parents' bedroom and started tearing it apart. They threw clothes out of the closets and ripped off the boards joined to the wall. Threw their mattress onto the floor. I could hear others tearing up the kitchen and my brother's and my rooms upstairs.

"When they didn't find anything, they tied bags over my father's and brother's heads and took them with them. Outside, the neighbor's dog, a big German shepherd, came running up, barking. The Americans shouted at the dog to shut up, and when it started snarling at them, one of them shot it. But didn't kill it. The dog was squealing and writhing on the ground as they drove away.

"My father told me later the soldiers drove for about twenty minutes, then unloaded him and my brother into a group of other men they'd rounded up. He couldn't tell where they were. The men had to sit on the ground for five hours with the bags on their heads, no water, no food, no toilets. When some of them finally had to go to the toilet in their pants, the Americans called them stinking Arabs. Then they loaded them onto another truck and drove them to a prison, not Abu Ghraib, but somewhere on an American base.

"My father was put in a big cell with twenty other older men and one broken toilet, only the floor to sleep on. Every couple of days they would interrogate him again, asking who he knew in the insurgency, where weapons were stored. Sometimes they would try to scare him into thinking he'd be tortured if he didn't give names. They tied his hands and blindfolded him and turned on an electric saw next to his ear. The sound was terrifying, he said, but they didn't actually cut him. He kept insisting he didn't know anything and the raid on our house was a mistake because of the mix-up of names.

"After two weeks they let him go and offered him a job as an interpreter because his English was so good. He wanted to scream at them, 'Get out of my life, get out of my country,' but was afraid to. He just said no.

"The Americans tortured my brother, maybe because he'd fought back at the house. They stripped him naked, tied wires to his toes, and sent electric shocks through him, then asked him for names of people in the resistance. When he didn't give them, they stepped up the current. He said it was a kind of pain he'd never experienced before. It took over his body like an invading force and sent his legs and arms wild, making him thrash around the floor while the Americans laughed at him. He felt as if his blood was boiling and his skin would explode. Then they threw buckets of ice-cold water on him. That almost gave him a heart attack. When he still wouldn't talk, they told him would tie the wires to his penis. But they didn't. They just sent him back to this big crowded cell and brought in the next man.

"My brother was actually expecting to be tortured more, but there were so many prisoners, and the Americans had to concentrate on the ones they most suspected. Those poor guys really got it — attacked with dogs when they were naked, no sleep, almost drowned, hung from hooks on the wall, beaten, drugged. He saw some of them afterwards — shattered, half crazy, the only things holding them together were hatred of the Americans and love of Allah.

"After a month they let my brother go. He came back different, much more quiet and distant. A tenderness he'd had before was gone. In its place was a bitter determination and a hard-earned pride that he hadn't given in, they hadn't broken him, he hadn't told about our cousin. He was harsh, and I didn't feel as close to him. But I loved and respected him.

"I could tell the humiliation our family had suffered was weighing on him. In our culture such things demand retaliation. That is how their effect is undone. Otherwise they remain a stain on the soul. My brother knew it was his duty to restore the family's honor as well as his own. My father is old and my mother and I are women. We cannot be expected to make the reprisals ourselves.

"A few days after he was released, he went searching for our cousin, to join him in the resistance. Ahmad had heard he was in prison, and he said as soon as he saw my brother, he knew that he hadn't betrayed him. Ahmad had seen many men come back from torture. The ones who didn't break were proud and wanted to become long-term fighters. The ones who had talked were crushed and wanted to become suicide bombers to redeem themselves. The insurgency needs and honors both men. The ones who talked under torture are accepted back without accusation because everyone knows it could be them next time. Their desire for martyrdom is respected.

"My brother had no military training. I don't think he'd ever fired a gun. Ours isn't that sort of family. But firing a gun is a simple thing, and he got good at it. Baghdad now has so many gutted buildings, and those give good cover for snipers. But it's very boring work, he said. You have to wait and watch for hours before you get a target — some days you never get one. The best targets are the convoys, but they're always changing their routes for protection. Because of their fear, they tear through the streets at top speed, forcing other cars off the road, running over pedestrians, never stopping. He talked about how good it feels to spray the trucks with your Kalashnikov and see the invaders falling over. You have to shoot and run, though, because they sometimes have helicopters with them, and they'll blow up your building with a rocket.

"When he's out on the street, he carries a hidden pistol. A couple of times he's been able to follow an American patrol and shoot into their backs, then disappear into the crowd. The Americans open fire in all directions. He's sorry about the killed civilians, but this is the only way to drive out the invaders.

"The other reason he carries the pistol is to keep from being taken prisoner. If he's ever surrounded, he'll kill as many soldiers as he can and save the last shot for himself. He's determined not to be captured and tortured again because he knows next time will be worse, and he's not sure he can take it.

"He doesn't know how many he's killed and wounded, but it's enough so that the family's honor is again intact. But he wants to continue the battle. He's now fighting the Americans on a larger scale where he can use his education. He's in Iran working as a physicist. They are developing smaller, cheaper heat-seeking missiles to shoot down US aircraft.

"He says the main advantage the Americans have is their Air Force. Their soldiers don't really believe in what they're doing and don't want to take risks in battle. Their main motivation is just to survive and go home, and you can't win wars that way.

"But the USA controls the air. Their planes and helicopters can destroy a whole area, and they don't mind killing everybody in it.

"Heat-seeking missiles are now bulky and expensive, but he and the other scientists are researching ways to micro-miniaturize the sensors and mass produce them in guidance systems. He says being able to shoot down their planes will totally change the balance of power. They'll have to fight us face to face, and they'll lose that way.

"I haven't seen my brother in a year and a half. When we said good-bye, he seemed like someone else. His gentleness had been replaced by hatred and the need for vengeance. I love him and feel sorry for what he's been through and worry he'll be killed, but I don't feel very comfortable with him. Violence warps people.

"He calls his project SAMs for Uncle Sam and thinks it's a great idea. But I call it the ongoing insanity of the arms race and think it's a terrible idea. It'll just force the Americans to develop some new kind of horrible weapon that will kill even more people.

"We somehow have to get out of this whole way of thinking. We have to realize that war doesn't solve problems, just creates new ones. It generates more rage that then breaks out again in violence. With all the atomic weapons, we'll end up turning this lovely planet into a mass graveyard, not just for humans but for everyone except radiation-resistant insects."

"Some people say fighting these small wars is a way to prevent a nuclear war. Or attacking another country is necessary to prevent them from attacking us."
"Those are murderous lies. Every war is sold to us as a preventive war. That's a favorite claim of tyrants, and I think some of them really believe it, that we're being threatened by savages and have to strike against them. It's a projection of their own personality. Hitler said he was protecting Western civilization from the Russian hordes. Saddam demonized the Iranians to scare us into war with them, just as Bush demonized the Iraqis. I've been reading about the Vietnam War. The hawks kept saying, 'If we don't fight the Communists in Vietnam, we'll have to fight them in California. They're trying to destroy us any way they can.' But it wasn't true. The opposite was true. The Communists were trying to build a different economic system, so the capitalists wanted to destroy *them* any way they could. Warmongers have always portrayed themselves as the only alternative to the brutal beasts out there. They generate fear to stay in power.

"One favorite trick of the USA is to secretly support the reactionary side in a civil war with arms and money. If their side starts to lose, they suddenly get upset about this awful war and all the people who are dying. They say they need to intervene for humanitarian reasons, to bring peace and prevent a holocaust. Then they jump in openly and try to crush the other side."

"The war that's going on now, how do you see that ending?"
"Disaster for the Americans. They started this war, and they deserve to lose it. They think they can win with all their money and weapons, but our people are stronger than that. We will continue to fight and resist for as long as it takes to defeat the invaders and their figurehead government.

"These so-called Iraqi Security Forces are only there for the money. They don't believe in the cause. They won't fight and die for the Americans, they'll just take their money and run.

"The more people the Americans kill, they more enemies they create. They can't kill all the people. The people are stronger. We have them surrounded, and they're afraid to come out of their bases, just like in Vietnam. We're going to drive them out of the country, get rid of their Arab pawns, and take back our land — oil and all. We are a patient people, and the Americans are impatient.

"One reason they are impatient is because deep down they know what they're doing in Iraq is wrong. They can ignore that for a while, but not forever. It eats away at them. They are human too. They know they would react to an invasion they same way we are. They don't have the heart for this fight, but we do. This is our home. We will win.

"But the tragic thing is that it won't end there, either for Iraq or America. The violence the USA has unleashed will continue in both countries. That's the way of barbarity. It doesn't just stop, it keeps going on in different ways. The war may be over, but people on both sides have been infected with the disease of cruelty, and it spreads. It gets passed on, finding new victims who then turn into attackers and contaminate others with it. Violence really is a plague, and since the Americans inflicted it on us, they must bear the brunt of it — killings, crime, chaos in their society. They must suffer as much as the suffering they have caused. That is the divine justice."

"Do you see any cure to this disease?"

"Sure. Give the UN the power to keep the peace. For instance, the American invasion of Iraq is a clear violation of the UN Charter, but the UN can't do anything about it. They need enough power to outlaw invasions and other acts of war and to enforce that with economic and political sanctions strong enough to work. They could outlaw the manufacture and possession of military weapons — from assault rifles to nuclear bombs. Governments could take some of the money they spend on the military and put it into an international peace fund that would inspect world-wide for weapons and destroy them. No more military training. Send the soldiers home.

"I'm not saying there wouldn't be problems and conflicts, but they would end up killing far fewer people. We would need to expand the World Court and give it jurisdiction to settle disputes between countries and groups of people. Conflicts would be decided by laws, not force. That's called civilization, and it works pretty well within countries. Now we need to make it work between countries. That'll be difficult, but we can do it ... we have to."

"Would you make people give up their personal weapons?"
"With a license they could have a pistol for protection and a simple rifle for hunting. You can't kill huge numbers of people with those."

"Your idea sounds definitely worth trying."
"Think of the lives and money that would save. But the politicians and corporate executives don't want it. They want to use the military to build their empire and hold on to power. That's more important to them than peace. *Their* children don't die in the wars.

"Governments and corporations have become enemies of the people. We need to take their power away. We can't let them keep killing. All of us are their potential victims now. Having gone from being ruled by Saddam Hussein to George W. Bush, I can tell you we need a whole other approach to politics. There's no real difference between those two men. They're both murderers.

"That's why the USA helped Hussein into power in the first place. They knew he would control Iraq with an iron fist and would never nationalize the oil. They kept him in power with massive military aid. Hussein was just a marionette of the USA who had the audacity to cut his strings and act on his own, so naturally the USA had to string him up.

"This kind of interference is the main reason America and Britain are so hated in the world. That's why there's terrorism. People are sick and tired of being abused, of having their politics manipulated and their economies controlled from the outside. Arabs have had it up to here with this new colonialism that the West is using to control our oil. We refuse to be dominated anymore, and we're resisting with the only weapon we have — guerrilla warfare."

"What about the Arab leaders who are on the US side?"
"These so-called leaders represent only the comprador[8] elite in their countries. They serve Western interests and are hated by the people. They stay in office only with their Western arms.

"But it can't last. The USA and the rich Arabs are doomed. Bush blew the whole show by creating too many enemies. Billions of people now oppose the USA. The USA can't kill them all. Before Bush, the American goal of a world empire was camouflaged with diplomacy, harder to see. But his stupidity turned out to be a boon to humanity. He made the plans obvious to everyone, so mass resistance coalesced. Obama's job is to restore the camouflage, but it's too late.

"I'm proud to be an Arab because we're at the forefront of this opposition. We're standing up to the most powerful military machine the world has ever seen ... and defeating it. Forty years ago the Vietnamese did it, and now we're doing it.

"Maybe finally the Americans will learn not to try to rule over other countries. That would be a big step towards peace."

8 Commercial agent for a foreign business.

— 14 —

The Split

Stan and Hannah Cooper are old friends of mine from college days. Back then we were three malcontents alienated from the mainstream, so we drew together in mutual defense and support. Hannah was the most politically active of us and was always dragging Stan and me to demos and abstruse lectures on Trotskyism. She went to law school, became a public defender, and is currently a criminal defense attorney. Stan became a high school teacher and recently took early retirement because of an ulcer. Although we've changed over the years, we've managed to stay in close communication.

I introduced them to each other and attended their wedding, so I've felt attached not just to them but also to their marriage. When Stan recently told me they were planning to divorce, I was shocked and saddened. Hoping to talk them out of this, I persuaded them to take part in a three-way phone call to hash out their differences and hopefully see that those are less important than the bond they've built together over all these years. When it turned out that their differences have a lot to do with the topic of this book, they agreed to let me publish excerpts from the recording we made.

Hathaway: *"You two mean a lot to me, and you mean a lot to each other, probably more than you're aware of now in the midst of your conflict."*
Stan: "We're aware of that, but it doesn't help much. Sure, we've been through a lot together, the world's been through

a lot, and all that has changed us both, but now we're quite different people from who we were back then when we got married. It's sort of, 'That was then, this is now.' And 'now' doesn't seem to work between us anymore. The main thing we have in common now is that we're both unhappily married. But since it's to each other, it doesn't help much."
Hannah: **"Of course we've both changed, but you've changed enormously, Stan. You've done a one-eighty."**
"I don't see it that way."

"Let's talk about these changes. What gets me is that, well, from our other conversations it seems that your differences aren't really about the two of you as people. They're more about your opinions on external issues. The question I have is, How important can opinions be?

"Look at it this way, you've been married forty years, you've raised two kids to successful adulthood and families of their own. The hard part is over. If you could make it through all that, how can some differences of opinion drive you apart now?"
"I wouldn't classify these just as opinions. These are very basic matters. The life or death of many people is hanging in the balance of these issues. This is not abstract."

"Well, let's lay it all out on the table and take a look. I understand it has a lot to do with Israel."
"It starts with Israel and goes from there."
"It goes from there all the way to another Holocaust. If you have your way, if the people you support come to power in Israel and the USA, they'll stop resisting the terrorists and become holier-than-thou pacifists while the Arabs push the Jews into the sea and blow up half the USA. Then the pacifists will cry about what a tragedy it all is.

"Well, I'm not going through another tragedy. I'm not going to see America and Israel destroyed because we didn't have the courage to stand up to fanatics. I'm not going to have our generation go through something like our grandparent's went through. Once is enough, once was way too many, and now we have to finally defend ourselves."

"No way am I in favor of pushing the Jews into the sea. Whenever we talk about this, you exaggerate my position. You get very thin-skinned and go into your attack mode."

"Yeah, I admit, I and lots of other Jews are thin-skinned about this issue. But when you think about how many Jewish skins got stretched over lampshades not so long ago, it's understandable that we might feel a tad oversensitive. My grandmother's brother, my great uncle, got gassed in Auschwitz. And her cousin got shot in the neck in Sachsenhausen.

"You know I lost family too. They didn't even make it to the concentration camps. They were murdered in the Kiev ghetto by the German SS. I'm not playing this down. I've got relatives in Israel just like you do, and I don't want them killed. But the Zionists have tunnel vision about this issue. They focus just on one part of it — preventing another Holocaust, no matter what. But I'm convinced that what the Zionists are doing now is making another *Shoah*[9] more likely. Their moral compass has got thrown off by the trauma they went through. It's making them do things that violate the basic principles of Jewish ethics. The moral sensitivity, the qualities that make me most proud to be a Jew are getting destroyed by these Israeli militarists."

"Self defense isn't unethical. The Torah never said lie down and let people kill you. We have to survive. If we're attacked, we have to fight back."

"Oh, ugh, William. Stan and I have been through this so many times before. Do we really have to drag all this stuff out again? What's the point?"

"Think of this as the dump truck part of it. You just pour everything out, say everything again, heap it all up in front of you both. I know it's unpleasant, but trust me. This is going somewhere."

"Well, I'll dump this. Hannah pooh-poohs anti-Semitism, says, 'It's not so bad anymore; don't be paranoid.' But the fact is it's getting much stronger, and that's worldwide.

"I'll give you an example of something that happened to me just last year. I walked into my classroom one morning,

9 Holocaust.

and someone had written 'Jews are dog shit' on the board. Some students were already in the room, and they all said it was there when they got there. I erased it, but next day it was there again, 'Jews are dog shit.' Nobody saw who did it, or so they claimed. It kept happening a couple of times a week. The students still played dumb. I thought they really knew who was doing it, but I couldn't prove it. I'd get there early, trying to catch them at it, but never could. I asked the janitors to check the room, but I don't think they actually did. They didn't really care.

"One night about ten o'clock, the doorbell rang at home. I opened the door, and a fire was burning on the front porch, a brown paper bag going up in flames. The porch is wood. I was afraid the whole house would catch fire. When I stomped out the blaze, I found out the bag was filled with dog shit, got it all over my shoes.

"Next morning I go into the classroom, and on the board is 'Jews house burn like dog shit.' Students just sitting there. And of course whoever did it didn't even make it grammatical, and it was an English class.

"I asked the police to watch the house, but they said they didn't have the manpower for that. All I could do was get new smoke alarms, install motion detectors, leave lights burning all night in the yard, and increase the fire insurance on the house. Do you know what it's like trying to fall asleep in a house that might burn down any night? I was afraid to take sleeping pills because I might not hear the smoke alarm. I was a wreck, and nobody gave a damn. Not even you, Hannah. You said it was just a prank."

"I said it was a *vicious* prank. But no, I didn't think they'd actually burn down the house. They'd already achieved what they were after — they'd made your life miserable."

"Well, Jews are tired of having their lives made miserable. Far worse anti-Semitic attacks than this are happening all over the world. The neo-Nazis are on the rise in Germany. Jews get beaten up in Russia. Synagogues in Paris and Rome have to be guarded by the police. All this proves that the Jews need a secure homeland, a place they can go where they'll be safe.

"And seeing how most of the world doesn't give a damn if Israel lives or dies, that changed me. I stopped being a left-winger when I saw how they fawn over the Palestinians. They make excuses for al-Qaeda. They defend Iran. And they oppose the only progressive, democratic country in the Mideast. Left-wingers have lost whatever meaning they ever had, so I'm not one of them anymore."

"How would you classify yourself now politically?"
"I'm that most despised of all creatures, a liberal. 'Live and let live' is my political platform. I've given up on ideologies. Don't get me wrong, though — I definitely haven't become a right-winger. I think George W. Bush was the worst president we ever had."
"Here's another of our differences. I think he was the best president we ever had."

"That's quite a statement, Hannah. If Bush was the best, then who was the worst?"
"Lincoln, because he killed more of us than any other president. I'm not talking about him as a person, I'm talking about his policies. He slaughtered over a half-million Americans to preserve national power, to make sure the USA would dominate the continent. That's monstrous. Human beings don't exist to serve the state. They are the state."

"Then why do you think Bush was the best?"
"Because he shattered the carefully constructed illusion that the USA is a benevolent country with good intentions for the world. This was just a PR image, but many people, especially at home, believed it. Bush stripped away this façade and showed everyone that the USA is intent on empire. He exploded the myth of good heartedness that had been built up over the years. The world owes him a debt of gratitude, because now the multitudes are rising to defend themselves."
"You see, William, how can you talk to someone like that, let alone live with her? Lincoln the worst president and Bush the best — ridiculous!"

"Well, I'm not so fond of sharing my bed with a liberal. But I've always been on the left side of the bed, so I'm willing to stay with it.

"As for your change of politics, I admit I don't think much of liberalism. Or any mainstream electoral politics. Remember what Emma Goldman said, 'If elections could change anything, they'd be illegal.'

"American elections are more entertainment than politics. The campaigns are like boxing matches ... actually more like mud wrestling. A ritual to choose a group parent-figure we can identify with ... or a tribal totem who embodies our feelings. It's just drama, an emotional diversion from the real political issues.

"The emphasis is on the personality of the candidate, who's portrayed as someone we would like and who would like us — a powerful friend who thinks and feels like us and will make our lives better. By showing everything through a lens of emotion, the media infantilize the political discourse. That's of course to make us more malleable and make us avoid analysis of the power structures that determine our lives. Very useful.

"It seems to me that both candidates actually represent the corporations, the true power holders. We get to choose which of two corporate spokespersons we want. But the corporations aren't a monolithic bloc. Some businesses are more consumer oriented — they favor the Democrats. Others are more monetary oriented — they favor the Republicans. There's lots of conflict between them. The president has to mediate all this and keep the game on track. No simple job, serving all those interests — none of which are ours."

"Hannah is running her tapes again. She's got her theory all worked out, and now she's on her soapbox."

"My dear husband, I'm just trying to save you from the delusions of liberalism. I'm convinced it exists to prevent basic change. It talks about gradual reforms, but they never amount to anything. They're just an illusion to distract us from the probability that for the rest of our lives we'll live under a business-dominated government

in an increasingly degraded society. This thought is so painful that rather than accept it, we'll grasp at any straw of hope. And that's all the liberals are selling us.

"Going along with them prevents us from laying the groundwork for long-term fundamental change. Better if we don't buy their false hope. Then we can focus on the kind of radical action that could lead to major change in fifty years. I think that's the kind of time frame the oligarchy is worried about. They know they've got the near term sewn up, so they want to keep us focused there.

"She's quite an orator, isn't she? Very eloquent. She's practiced it a lot. I've heard it all before. I keep telling her she should run for president — on the anarchist ticket.

"The thing is, Hannah, we live in the near term. It's only human that we'd want it to be better."

"That's why liberals are so successful. 'Things are terrible now,' they say, 'but vote for us and they'll be better ... in few years.' Young people believe that. Naturally they want to think their future looks good. But I've been hearing it all my life ... and the conditions under which working people live haven't got better. Corporate profits have got better while wages have got worse. The rich are getting richer and the poor are getting poorer ... and the middle are getting fewer. That's under liberal presidents as well as conservative ones. They're all on the same team. And it's not our team."

"You were captain of the debate team, as I remember. Now you've become a real pro at it.

"But your kind of us-against-them thinking just leads to more polarization. There's too much of that already, it's tearing the country apart."

"Situations need to be polarized before they can change. That's why politicians say they want to heal the polarization — it's threatening to the status quo they're trying to preserve. But what we actually need is more polarization. That's the only way to get rid of the stand-pat center that keeps things as they are."

"That's how we could end up with a police state."

“That’s started already, it’s just happening gradually so we don’t react to it. We’d be better off if it were sudden — that would mobilize more rebellion, make it easier to defeat. Like that horrible experiment with the frogs. If you put a frog into boiling water, he’ll hop right out. But if you put him into normal water and slowly turn up the heat, he’ll stay there and die. The American people won’t stand for a quick shift to tyranny, but they’ll go along with it if it’s slow. At first it won’t be directed at them, and by the time it is and they revolt, it’ll be too late — the mechanisms will all be in place. Bush’s mistake was turning up the heat too fast, so now Obama will turn it down a bit. That’s why radicals need to sharpen the conflict now, to keep this gradual approach from taking hold.

“When we try to break the corporate power lock, they’ll react with repression. Sometimes things have to get worse before they can get better.

“I’d rather have a vivid life of opposing the powers. To go along with them in hopes of having it easier is collaboration, a living death.

“A crackdown would help us see how much we have in common with workers in poor countries who’ve been bearing the brunt of globalized capitalism. We can finally join with them instead of viewing them as a threat. When we work together, the oligarchs won’t be able to stop us. They’re too few. We’ll take control of the economic power that really belongs to us, and we’ll use it to build a world that’s fair for everyone. It might not be perfect, but it would be a lot better than what we have now.”

“Now she’s giving her closing arguments to the jury. But it’s pie in the sky. When you talk like that, Hannah, I feel like I’m in a time capsule back to 1968.”

“What’s wrong with that? Sure, since then there’s been a massive campaign to discredit these ideas, but they’re still true.”

“I believed them at the time, but now they seem empty rhetoric.”

“I think you’ve fallen for the conservative propaganda. They have a whole communications industry devoted to

convincing us that if we try to change this system, we'll end up with something much worse. They want us to believe our only alternatives are this or North Korea. But we've got lots of choices."

"The choices you favor are too much like Communism, and look what that led to — brutal dictatorship."

"I agree that Communism turned into something pretty terrible, but a lot of that was because it was always under attack. Right after the Russian Revolution the capitalist countries sent in troops trying to overthrow the new government. When that didn't work, they turned to sabotage, spying, economic warfare, and a constant military threat. They did everything they could short of world war to undermine and destroy this new system. Naturally that produced a siege mentality in the Soviet Union. A militarist like Stalin seemed the only way to defend the revolution.

"Another factor is that Russia, China and Cuba never had a tradition of democracy. When they came under assault, they fell back into totalitarianism. But if they hadn't been attacked, they might have built something quite different.

"As it was, they never achieved anything close to real socialism. All they got was state capitalism where the government became the boss and the workers were still powerless.

"Now we can learn from their mistakes and do it better. A country with a tradition of democracy can build a whole other kind of socialism — libertarian and decentralized. We can eliminate the economic conflict that leads to war, replace it with sharing and cooperation. The world could turn into quite a wonderful place to live."

"Or a living hell. I don't think our freedoms would last under something like that."

"They're not lasting now. They don't apply to everyone anymore, only to those who don't rock the boat. You remember what happened to that client of mine?"

"Right. The Arab again."

"What happened?"

"He was an agricultural science student from Morocco and spoke at an anti-war demonstration here on campus, everything legal and peaceful. The police photographed him and got the university to let them examine their file photos of foreign students. The cops identified him and searched his dormitory room, where they found a Koran, prayer rug, some ammonium fertilizer, and several Arabic language magazines, one of which had a picture of Osama bin Laden. They confiscated his computer and found he had the al-Jazeera website bookmarked and had written e-mails to people in Morocco with insulting comments about the American president. They searched his car and found a timer from a clothes dryer. And with that they arrested him for violating the Patriot Act. Front page story in the paper: 'Terror Suspect Arrested, Bomb Materials Found.'

"It turned out the fertilizer was for a research project he was doing, measuring plant growth rates with different types of ammonium. He had just a small amount, not enough to make a real bomb even if he'd wanted to. He took me to the greenhouse and showed me the project — twenty little pots of plants and charts for how much they're growing.

"He was working in a coin laundry near the campus, doing everything from cleaning up to simple repairs. The timer on one of the dryers was broken, so he'd taken it out. He couldn't fix it, so he called the main office, and they told him to bring it in and they'd give him a new one. He put it in his car, where the cops found it.

"They had no case at all, and it wasn't hard to convince the district attorney of that. The university confirmed his research project, an explosives expert confirmed that the amount of fertilizer was too small, and the laundry company confirmed they'd told him to bring in the broken timer.

"The DA told the cops he was going to drop the charges, but they said they had an additional lead and

needed another search warrant. They got it, and when they searched his room this time, they 'found' cocaine.

"This student was a devout Muslim, not the cocaine type at all, very traditional and old fashioned, like *yeshiva*[10] school-boys used to be. I'm one hundred percent certain the cops planted the drugs. They were determined to get him on something. He was an Arab speaking out against the war and saying unflattering things about the president. That meant he was an enemy and had to be got rid of.

"The DA didn't want to believe the city's finest would set someone up, but he did offer that if the student turned in his visa and left the country in two weeks, he'd drop the charges.

"I hated to go along with this deal, but I knew the kid didn't have a chance of getting a fair trial. He agreed and told me terrible stories about how other students had treated him. He left the USA bitter at having his education snatched away from him because of ignorant prejudice."

"Like I said at the time, I'm glad you helped the guy. You saved him from jail. And all pro bono.

"I think it's terrible when innocent people get swept up in all this. But what about all the innocent Israelis who are dying and the three thousand innocent Americans in 9/11? You don't seem to care about them."

"This idea that Israelis and Americans are innocent victims of terrorists is a myth. It's created to justify our aggression. Just like the belief that Islamic fundamentalists are the main terrorists in the world. It's Orwell's Big Lie. The USA and Israel started this battle. We've been abusing the Arabs in all sorts of ways for decades. We're the main terrorists. For every American killed in 9/11, we've already killed a hundred Muslims, and more every day. It's the same in Israel.

"The targets of 9/11 were soldiers in the Pentagon and financial managers in the World Trade Center. Both those groups are terrorists, just a subtler kind of terror. We

10 Jewish institution for study of Torah and Talmud, generally open to boys and men.

don't see it that way here, we just reap the benefits. We're conditioned to think of that as normal. But what the global poor suffer under our corporations and the International Monetary Fund and World Bank is economic terror. And what they suffer under military dictatorships supported by the Pentagon is physical terror.

"Even things that seem harmless to us like missionaries, pop music and movies become a form of cultural terrorism in a traditional society. The garbage that Hollywood is pouring into those countries is debasing their culture, just like it has ours. We're used to it, but they don't want to get used to it.

"When Muslims fight back against us, we label them terrorists. But terrorism means intentionally killing innocent civilians, and the financial manipulators and Pentagon officers aren't innocent.

"But no one deserves to be killed, innocent or not. Bombing anybody is barbaric and abhorrent. The USA and Israel are dropping bombs all the time, though, and the civilians they kill are just collateral damage to them. If we do it, we have to expect that people will do it to us. Violence creates counter-violence.

"From the Arab point of view, the Israelis are invaders, millions of Europeans who are pushing them off their land. It's like what happened in America. Millions of Europeans poured in and pushed out the people who were living here. The natives defended themselves by attacking white wagon trains and settlements, killing everyone they could — men, women and children. The whites called them terrorists, savages.

"Now the Arabs are fighting back. But like the Indians, their weapons aren't nearly as powerful as the Europeans'. What was it Mike Davis said? 'The car bomb is the poor man's air force.' The rich have Stealth bombers, the poor have Toyota Corollas, both filled with explosives. The bombers are a lot bigger and kill many more people.

"One of the reasons the Western powers supported the formation of Israel was that they thought the Arabs were

passive, they wouldn't defend themselves. But they've surprised us. They may win."

"William, as a Gentile, you can't imagine how offensive it is to me to hear drivel like this, especially from a fellow Jew ... and one I'm married to."

"You're right, I probably can't."

"Well, we're supposed to lay all our differences out on the table, so here they are.

"Don't think, though, that I'm singling out the Jews with this. They're no worse than any other European group. Western civilization has produced more violence than any other. Our history is a chronicle of atrocities. From the Romans on, it's been ghastly. We make Genghis Khan look like a pacifist. That's why I think our day is passing — we've harmed too many other peoples, and now we deserve to go under.

"But what breaks my heart is that before this the Jews hadn't been cruel and militaristic. We were peaceful. But we've become just as vicious as the *goyim*.[11] What a loss! Now it's obvious that the diaspora was a blessing. We were freed of the disease of nationalism. Now we're dying of it.

"I admit that after what they'd been through, it was understandable that the Zionists would feel they needed their own country and it should be around Jerusalem. They grew up reading in the Torah that God personally gave them that land. They're convinced it's theirs forever. And every Passover they vow, 'Next year in Jerusalem.' They're fixated on this area, even though it hasn't been theirs for two thousand years.

"But the fact that it's understandable doesn't make it right. It doesn't justify what they've done to the Arabs to get the land. Their own suffering has blinded them to the suffering they're causing others. That's what makes it so tragic.

"There are hundreds of ethnic groups in the world that don't have their own country. But if we needed our own, the land should have been taken from the Germans. That

11 Gentiles.

would've been fair. The Arabs didn't have anything to do with the Holocaust or with the expulsion by the Romans.

"For the Zionists, Israel was a wonderful dream — a place where Jews could be safe and our culture could flourish. But it's a terrible reality — war and the oppression of another people."

"Do you see any way out?"

"Well, I do. But this could be just wishful thinking, trying to see a glimmer of good in all this grief. It seems to me that this horrible insoluble dilemma is generating a crux of pressure, a desperate energy that may be able to spring humanity into its next stage."

"And what might that be? Pray tell."

"I know this sounds grandiose and impossible, but so have a lot of major shifts in human development right before they happened. I'm hoping this is the start of our species finally outgrowing its need for group identities. Having all these groups — familial, tribal, ethnic, national — leads to battles. But now we may be getting ready to view humanity as one unified group. We could be going through the birth pains of a new era in which we realize the whole world is our family.

"This terrible knot of problems in Israel/Palestine comes from group identities — religion, ethnicity, nationalism. It seems to be a knot that can't be untangled, so we'll have to cut through it. We'll have to start cutting loose from these identities, leaving them behind, dismantling the structures, stop thinking of ourselves as Jews and Arabs, Israelis and Palestinians, get beyond the whole deadly game of separation. This might be a long, slow process, but now is the time to start. Every step we can make in that direction will help. There's no other way out.

"The problems around Jerusalem are really a microcosm of the problems of the world. Since they're most intense there, that's where the breakthrough can happen. Whatever we can do to reduce the separating identities — tear down national boundaries, dissolve

ethnicity, eliminate the gap between rich and poor — will bring us closer to being a human family. I'm not saying do away with differences, just divisions.

"The separations have developed out of fear, because primitive life was such a struggle and humans felt so weak and vulnerable. They needed groups to survive. But now we're at another level, and the groups have become a threat to our survival. We need to leave them behind before we can have world peace. The horrors of the Mideast could be forcing us all to this new evolutionary step."

"Hosanna, Hannah! Praise the Lord! And in the meantime Israel goes down the tubes."

"Maybe so, as the first of many obsolete nations to fall apart and evolve into something more humane, a world family."

"Very convincing. You're good at arguments. That's why you're a good attorney. You're especially good at defending murderers ... like Hamas and the PLO."

"First of all, I don't defend murderers, I defend people accused of murder. Second, I'm not defending terrorists, I'm just saying it's inevitable they would fight against the aggressors who've taken their land. Here's an interesting fact: Osama bin Laden's mother is a Palestinian refugee. That explains a lot."

"OK, counselor. Too bad you're not a divorce lawyer, we could save a bundle."

"About this divorce issue, I have to say that nothing I've heard here is a reason to end a marriage. I get the impression you're both taking the other person's opinions on these issues as a personal attack. Just because you disagree about some area of life doesn't mean you can't respect and care about each other. These are outer topics you're quarreling about, but you're taking them so personally."

"They may be outer to a Gentile, but to a Jew they go very deep."

"Only if you buy into all the baggage that goes along with that identity."

"I can't stop being a Jew. The world won't let me."

"But that's not all you are, it's not your whole life. There are areas of life that have nothing to do with religion and politics. And in those areas you two have proved you can get along. The things you have in common are really more important, but you don't notice them now. Once you split up, though, you'll notice them. When they're gone, you'll miss them deeply, but it'll be too late.

"Believe me, you don't have any idea what you're getting into with a divorce. I did it once, and I can tell you that kind of pain is something to avoid if at all possible. After forty years your hearts have grown together. This may be overshadowed now, but you're connected in all sorts of ways that you're not even aware of until you rip them out and feel the pain that takes their place. Over all these years you've become a unit, and even if you get divorced, you'll continue to be a unit, just a split-apart unit. Politics aren't important enough cause each other pain like that. No way."

"OK, William, you scared us. Now what?"

"Now you empty the trash."

"What do you mean?"

"You've just spewed out all this stuff that's dividing you. Now you mentally stuff it into garbage bags, seal them up, and toss them into the back of that big stinky garbage truck that just pulled up in front of your house. You get rid of this junk. You're finished with it. You have irreconcilable differences in this area, so you close it down. There's nothing more to be said. You don't talk about politics anymore. You don't watch the news together. You don't say things you know will hurt the other's feelings. Find another way to say it.

"Instead, you emphasize all the areas where you are compatible. List the things you like to do together, and do them more often. Talk about issues where you have opinions in common. And spend some time every day being physically tender to each other. Life is about being kind. That's more important than being right.

"If we're trying to build a better world, it can't be any better than the relationships we build with the people around us. If

we can't do it at home, we won't be able to do it in society either. It's not 'out there.' It's us. Like Gandhi said, 'We have to become the change we want to see in the world.'

"You need to empty the trash once a week so it doesn't build up. Sit down together and spend an hour talking about your relationship — problems, hurt feelings, misunderstandings. These are the issues you need to keep discussing, not politics. Really communicate your emotions to each other. Be honest about all the hurts, and work on forgiving and accepting each other. Tell each other what you really need, and make compromises so you can both get it. Then the love that's buried underneath all that stuff will come out again, you'll renew it. You'll see again the qualities about the other person that made you fall in love with them. They're still there.

"This forgiveness and reconciliation are the essence of peacemaking. If individuals, especially two who know each other as well as you do, can't manage that, then nations will never be able to."

"Guilt trip, William!"

"Sorry. But just try this for a year before you file those papers."

"A year? Long time. How about six months with a renewal clause? What do you think, Hannah?"

"I want to stay with you, you big oaf."

That was fourteen months ago. When I talked with them recently, both agreed they are communicating much better and are closer than they've been in years.

— 15—

Conscious Peace

My own quest for peace through the fields of gender studies, evolutionary biology, and techniques of consciousness.

As Trucker mentioned, the word "radical" comes from the Latin "radix," meaning "root." Ever since I was a kid, I've been trying to understand the roots of violence. I grew up confronted with it various forms, from classmate bullies beating me up because, being a year younger, I was smaller, to schoolroom duck-and-cover drills when we were trained to hide under our desks if we saw the flash of a hydrogen bomb out the window, to my alcoholic father with his wide leather belt. I hated violence but was also intrigued by it, needing to know what caused it, what made people that way. Somehow I sensed we had to understand it before we could eliminate it.

So in 1964 as the USA began to invade Vietnam, before the moral atrocity of that was clear to me, I joined the Special Forces to write a book about war. I thought of myself as an investigative reporter trying to uncover the psychological roots of war, the inner forces that drive us to slaughter. But my image as a neutral observer was self-delusion. In fact I was an agent of violence. I helped rip a country apart and damage its lovely people. In harming others, I harmed myself, and the effects are still going on, for them and me.

Since then my books and articles have centered on this theme, as do many of my nonwriting activities. It's become my beat, as they say in the newspaper business, and I've approached it from various angles, all with the goal of healing this pathology.

I left the Army filled with revulsion, fouled and contaminated by the hyper-masculinity of warfare. After three years in the Special Forces, maleness seemed a poison that could destroy our whole planet.

This savagery, I became convinced, is fostered by a cult of the fathers. Young men are taught to seek initiation into the hierarchy of male power, to prove they're worthy of belonging, to fight for the approval of the patriarchs.

I became an enemy of patriarchy, until I realized that the very idea of enemies is a patriarchal construct. Our culture has a deep need of enemies to justify its fear and aggression. We manufacture a steady stream of evil opponents.

I thought if we had more women in power, they would change the system, take the boys' lethal toys away from them, and build a more humane civilization based on their gentler feminine nature. Alas, the pro-military policies of women leaders — Margaret Thatcher, Golda Meir, Indira Gandhi, Jiang Qing, Condoleezza Rice, Angela Merkel, Hillary Clinton — have shown this to be naïve and simplistic. They ended up serving the system rather than challenging it.

Despite this disappointment, I'm still hopeful about women's potential to create a more peaceful world. I was glad to vote for Cynthia McKinney of the Green Party for president in 2008. She came out clearly for nonviolence while Obama was proving his macho credentials by supporting capital punishment and threatening to bomb Pakistan.

It also seems to me that we have a moral obligation to vote for the candidate we'd actually like to see in office. That's the only way democracy can function. The major parties frame electoral choices as the lesser of two evils in order to exclude alternatives and maintain their lock on power. The futility this engenders in voters also works to their advantage: People give up on politics and leave it to the "professionals."

Women have been at the forefront of the peace movement since its inception. But it's apparent by now that being female doesn't automatically make a person more peaceful.

I've come to believe that this idea of a gentle feminine nature was invented to limit female power. Why should women be more peaceful than men? Since they are often the victims of violence, enforced gentleness denies them the ability to defend themselves.

I now think that violence is a potential shared by both men and women, but our culture has restricted it and other forms of power to men and denied them to women. In a similar way the culture declares emotions to be a female domain and ridicules men for indulging in them.

Rather than a masculine nature and a feminine nature, what we really have is a human nature. But we've divided and polarized our human traits, assigning some to men and others to women, making us all incomplete, partial creatures. This segregation has exaggerated masculinity into brutish domination and femininity into pathetic dependency. As Stan Goff writes in his excellent book *Sex & War*, "Men are not from Mars and women are not from Venus. They've been exiled there from Earth."

If we can integrate our human characteristics, we'll break out of the binary male-female trap and discover that gender is not an either-or dichotomy but a spectrum of mutual qualities. By reducing the differences between women and men, we'll see that violence is a shared problem we need to solve together.

For a while, though, I didn't think it could be solved at all. I came under the sway of sociobiologists who claim that humans are intrinsically warlike, that we are genetically programmed to kill, that lasting peace just isn't possible. Believing that our genes and hormones determine our behavior provides a passive comfort. By surrendering to forces beyond our control, we avoid the difficult work of changing ourselves and our society.

This theory of inevitable war gained support with research in primatology. Field studies showed that chimpanzees make warlike raids on neighboring colonies. Since chimps are our close genetic relatives, this implied that we too are a warring species, that our evolutionary heredity determines these violent traits and condemns us to slaughter.

Prehistoric evidence seemed to corroborate this hypothesis. Archeologists have found mass graves with crude weapons and skeletons showing signs of systematic murder dating as far back 13,000 years.

Some scientists concluded from all this that war is hardwired into human nature. This has been the conviction of most military and governmental policy makers, and they were glad that research was apparently supporting them. If our biological heritage makes war unavoidable, then we need a strong military for defense. The fact that someone out there will always be plotting to attack us makes our standing armies and arsenals of weapons necessary. Without superior force we would be conquered. Adherents of this worldview could now claimed scientific confirmation of their military policies.

Most scientists weren't really saying that, however. They realized that the great majority of humans and chimpanzees live peacefully, that mass violence is the exception rather than the rule. They avoided biological determinism and spoke instead of potentialities for violent behavior.

Then further research led to a key discovery. Primatologists found that the chimps that invaded their neighbors were suffering from shrinking territory and food sources. Those with adequate resources didn't raid other colonies. The invaders were struggling for survival. Their aggression wasn't a behavioral constant but was caused by the stress they were under. Their genes gave them the capacity for violence, but the stress factor had to be there to trigger it into combat.

Human wars also are caused by stress. They are usually either fear-motivated struggles to grab more resources or acts of revenge for previous wars.

The new research indicates that if we can reduce stress, we can reduce war. Our biological nature doesn't force us to war, it just gives us the potential for it. Without stress to provoke it, violence can remain one of the many unexpressed capacities our human evolution has given us.

Militarists and others with a vested interest in war reacted to these new findings by saying we still need a strong military because stress is inevitable and we can never eliminate it. This assumption that stress is necessary to life is deeply entrenched. Anxiety is a mainstay of our society and a powerful tool for manipulating us. Military training puts recruits under great stress in order to rouse their primitive aggression. The media bombard us with atrocity stories about our current enemies to overload us with fear and convince us the villains need to be stamped out. Much of our education, sports, and urban life are charged with tension. Capitalism is based on conflict.

We've been indoctrinated to think all these are normal and natural, but they're really pathological. They damage life in ways we can barely perceive because they're so built into us. We've become stress addicts, but that doesn't mean we have to stay that way.

Stress causes war and then war causes more stress, which soldiers bring home with them as the toxic seeds of the next war. To function on the battlefield, soldiers have to shut off their trauma behind a wall of numbness and deny their fear and pain. They return home closed down emotionally, distanced from other people, afraid of intimacy. To them, the world is a threatening place, full of foes who must be defeated.

They pass this mentality on to their children, who grow up insecure, fearful, and defensive. Children project these feelings onto the world, which then takes on that appearance for them. The false security of weapons appeals to them; the thought of a military defending them is comforting; firm structures of authority seem necessary. War becomes normal. And they become a willing pool of recruits for the next time their rulers want to attack another country.

I returned from my generation's war laden with fear and anger, but I denied those emotions, burying them under an "I'm all right, Jack" attitude. I was tough, I could take it, I was a survivor. Within certain parameters I could function well, but when my superficial control broke down, I would fall into self-destructive depressions. I finally had to admit I was carrying a huge burden of stress, and I knew I had to get rid of that before I could live at peace with myself or anyone else.

My best friend from Special Forces, Keith Parker, had started doing Transcendental Meditation and said it made his mind clear and calm. I tried it and found he was right. When I meditated, I sat with eyes closed and thought a mantra, a sound without meaning that took my mind to quieter, finer levels and eventually beyond all mental activity to deep silence. Subjectively, TM was like diving down through an inner ocean into a realm of serenity. The effects were more real than anything I'd experienced through prayer or psychedelics. My stress and pressure began to be relieved.

I undertook more intensive practice and enrolled in a course to become a teacher of TM. During this time I had an experience of intense catharsis, referred to by TM's founder as "unstressing." I discuss this in more detail in the Afterword.

After my unstressing experience I felt so light and clear that I figured I'd totally recovered from being in the military. But I was wrong. Violent deeds require not just meditation but also atonement to heal them. I'd damaged much more than just myself — I'd damaged others and helped devastate a country. Such negative acts need to be balanced with positive ones. My experience in TM teacher training started the healing process, and in the months that followed I was able to confront what I'd done and accept responsibility for it.

This led to a phase of guilt that was painful but also therapeutic. I didn't need to condemn myself, but I did need to experience at least a fraction of the suffering we had inflicted on the Vietnamese and Cambodians. This was a period of contrition for me.

During that time I read about a Fellowship of Reconciliation project sending doctors and medicine to help in a small way to treat the health crisis we had created there. The violence we unleashed left hundreds of thousands of people crippled from wounds and amputations, burned into disfigurement, blinded by shrapnel, mentally traumatized. Rates of cancer and birth defects due to Agent Orange were soaring, and many watersheds and agricultural lands were still contaminated with this poison.

In the Paris Peace Accords the USA had promised humanitarian aid for the medical catastrophe we'd caused, but as soon as our soldiers were out, we refused to pay for it. We also refused to trade with Vietnam, plunging the country even deeper into an economic crisis.

Such depths of cruelty contradict the image of America we've been raised with, so most of us just shut our minds to it, preferring image to reality. But having been part of it, I couldn't shut my mind to it.

Knowing I had an obligation to help, I started donating to the project, first a few dollars a month, then more. The phrase "give till it hurts" kept popping into my mind, so I increased the amount until it was really a strain. At that point the feelings of guilt began to fade, replaced by a quiet resolve to do what I could to help.

I was learning a lesson in karma: If we hurt others, it comes back on us. There really is no "other"; we're basically the same, so it's ourselves we're hurting.

Another form of accepting pain is in the threat of prison that hangs over me for helping soldiers desert. I would really hate to be locked up in the gargantuan, egregiously inhumane, ever expanding US prison system. The thought of it scares me. So I guess that's one of the reasons I have to risk it. If I'm imprisoned, my experiences won't be nearly as bad as those of the Vietnamese I took prisoner and sent off to the tiger cages.

After the Vietnam War, it gradually became clear that our government had learned only tactical, not moral, lessons from it and was determined to continue a militaristic course, finding new ways to kill leftist rebels and strengthen rightist regimes around the world.

If Americans could acknowledge the ugly facts of our history, then go through a process of repentance and reparation for what we've done, this country could transform itself into the benevolent power it now pretends to be. This would be a long, painful process, but we could bring about a reconciliation that could lead to lasting peace. The money now spent on war could be used to remedy the sources of stress that cause it: poverty, prejudice, psychological trauma, the desire to dominate.

This transformation, however, is precisely what our government and its corporations want to prevent. War is essential to their economic power. So they rally us around the flag with mind-numbing patriotism and scare us with stories of evil enemies to recruit support for new wars against new demons. And the majority go along with this — because we're frightened, because we love our country, because we don't want to lose what little we have.

Barack Obama won the presidency by convincing us he would change things, but so did John Kennedy, Jimmy Carter and William Jefferson Clinton, and their changes amounted to little more than a fresher, friendlier image. The imperialist agenda remained the same. So far Obama's actions indicate he's not any different.

This is not surprising. Only politicians who have proved themselves loyal to the establishment can rise high enough in the Democratic Party to get nominated for major offices. Anyone who wants to move away from capitalism gets weeded out at the lower echelons.

Obama is increasing our troops in Afghanistan, expanding our air strikes in Pakistan, and using mercenaries to attack the resistance in Iraq. Refusing to accept defeat, he's determined to hold on to some degree of control in Iraq and Afghanistan. Despite his idealistic rhetoric, he serves the needs of empire, and in these times that means war. Controlling the oil supplies is too crucial and Muslim resistance is too strong for the fighting to end soon. As part of the "long war" strategy, we are shifting to proxies rather than GIs to fight it, outsourcing it to private contractors and local military. When American soldiers aren't dying, the war will disappear from the media and our minds. The sheep will believe it to be peace and fall gratefully back to sleep.

Before we can break this system's hold on us, we need to reject the mirage of change that liberals offer. Instead, I think we should focus on direct action that circumvents and vitiates the power of both parties. Our rulers aren't nearly as powerful as they want us to believe. We can take the power back, and the revitalizing effects of that will show us it was ours to begin with.

A good place to start would be a Property to the People movement. We organize rent and mortgage strikes: Stop paying landlords and banks for the right to live in our homes and instead reclaim that right for ourselves. As the resulting defaults overload the courts, we form No-Eviction Brigades. Whenever a family is about to be thrown out of its home, they are protected by hundreds of determined people who lock themselves on and defy the police with tactics of mutual defense. We can overwhelm them with our numbers; they can't throw us all out. Their attempts to do that will draw more people into the struggle and forge bonds of solidarity among us. Once we've reclaimed the property where we live, we'll be inspired to reclaim the property where we work and farm. We'll realize Woody Guthrie's truth: This land is our land.

Actions such as this can radicalize masses of previously uninvolved people and build a popular front with a broad social base. Once we start breaking the mechanisms of ownership, we'll see how these have bound and constrained our lives, forced us into making the owners wealthy with our labor. We'll realize the personal price we are paying for their prosperity.

But we need to overthrow this as nonviolently as possible, because, as Martin Buber pointed out, whatever violence we use will contaminate our new society, and the result may be another form of oppression, as the history of revolutions shows.

For it to be a real improvement, the new society must be built with an enlightened consciousness. In addition to social action, we need to work on ourselves, since individuals are the basic unit of society. The change has to be internal before it can be external. As the old 1960s bumper sticker said, “Peace begins within you.” The guiding principle of UNESCO also speaks to this: “Since war begins in the minds of men, it is in the minds of men that the defenses of peace must be constructed.”

Gandhi summed it up in *Nonviolence in Peace and War*: “There is no path to peace. Peace is the path.”

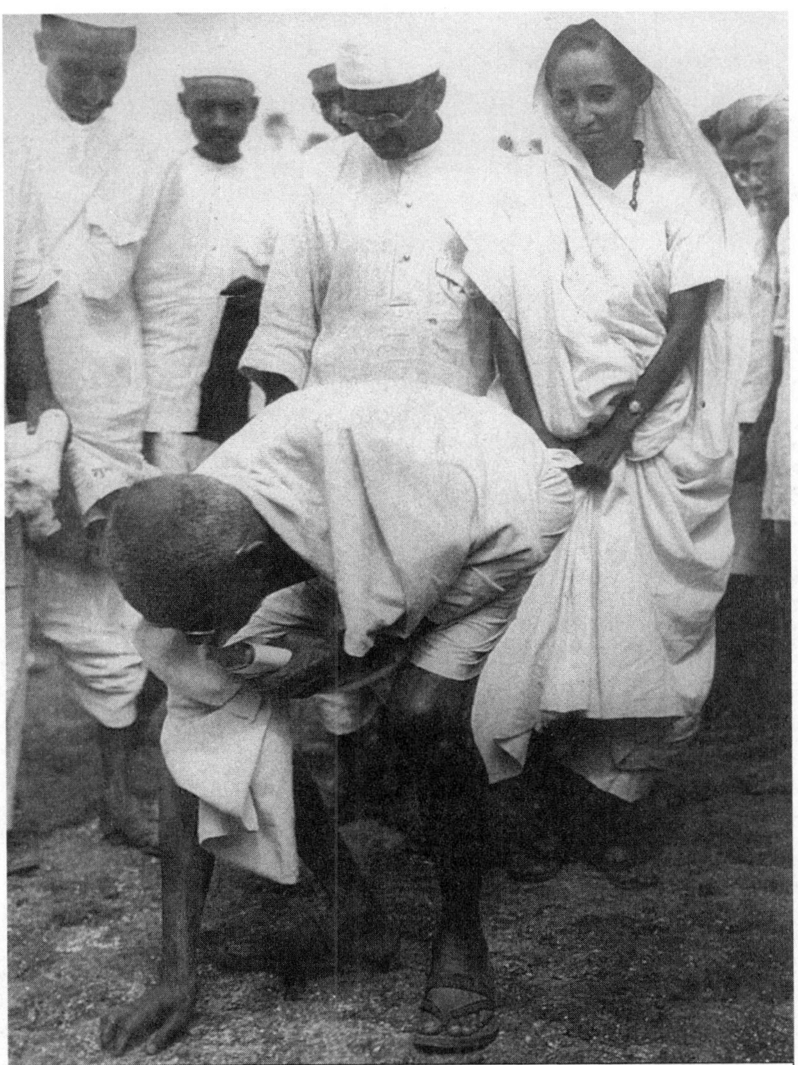

Joined by thousands on a march of almost 250 miles, on the morning of April 5, 1930, Mohandas Gandhi lifted a lump of salty mud. "With this, I am shaking the foundations of the British Empire," he declared. He then boiled the lump in seawater, producing illegal salt, and implored his followers to likewise begin making salt along the seashore "wherever it is convenient" and to instruct villagers in making illegal salt.

Mass civil disobedience spread throughout India as millions broke the salt laws by making salt or buying illegal salt. Salt was sold illegally all over the coasts of India. In reaction, the British government incarcerated over sixty thousand people by the end of the month. Millions saw the newsreels showing the march. *Time* magazine declared Gandhi its 1930 Man of the Year, noting that Gandhi marched to the sea "to defy Britain's salt tax as some New Englanders once defied a British tea tax."

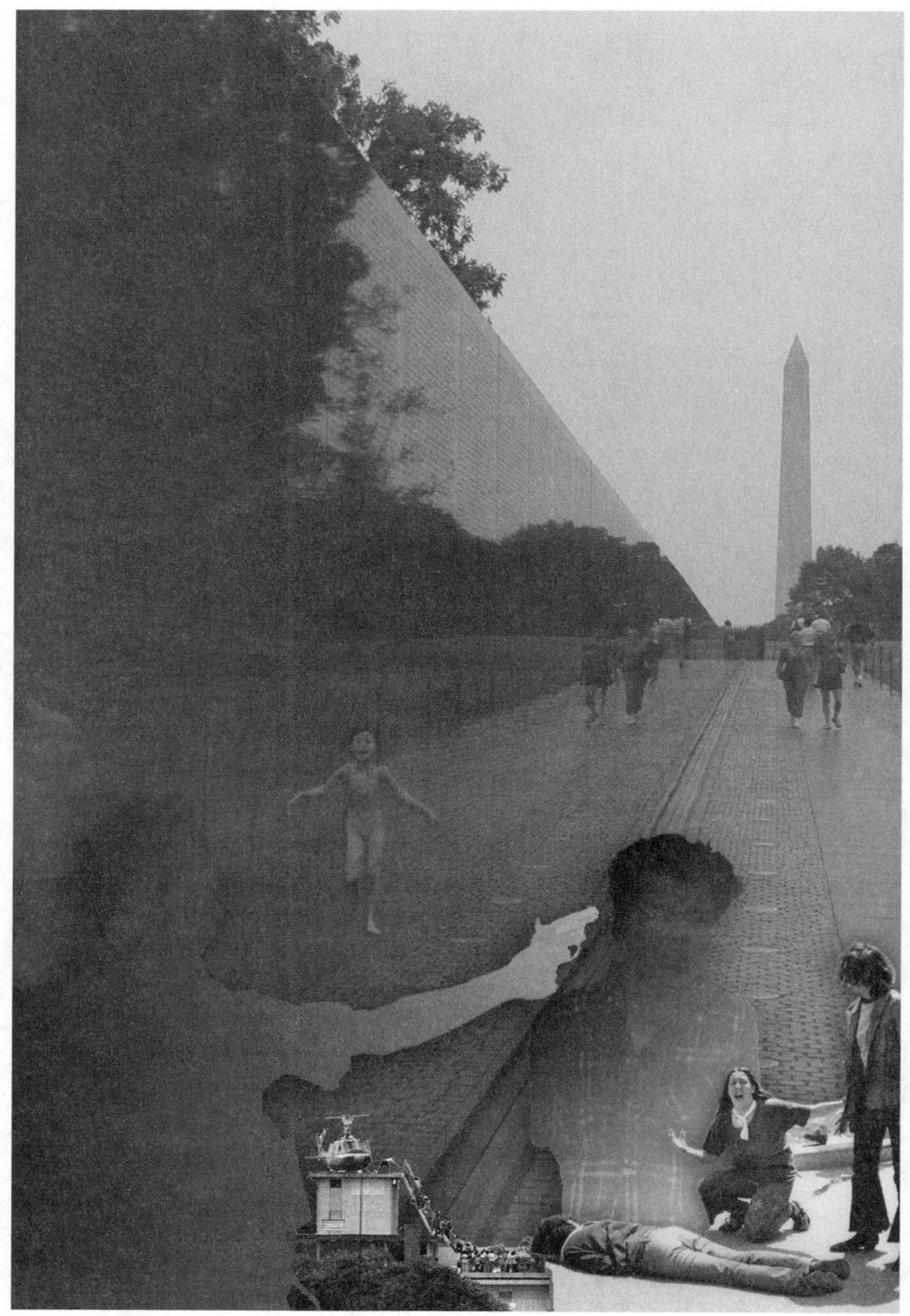

Afterword

All the contributors to this book hope you have appreciated these accounts of our experiences. Not all these approaches are appropriate for everyone, of course, but the greater the variety of tactics the peace movement can employ, the greater our chances for success. The traditional ways of petitions and marches remain important but are obviously not sufficient. New ways of opposing war are needed, and we wanted to share ours with you in hopes the movement can incorporate different methods and build a solidarity of diversities.

As discussed in the last chapter, my own journey toward peace was facilitated by my experiences with Transcendental Meditation. Not long after I began to meditate, I started going on World Peace Assemblies, large courses led by Maharishi Mahesh Yogi or one of his assistants where we meditated as a group. This strengthened the effects, making me feel both tranquil and energized. Then I attended a four-month course to learn to be a teacher of Transcendental Meditation. It was an amazing time. Every day we did hours of "rounding," repeating cycles of meditation, yoga asanas, and breathing exercises, each taking us deeper towards transcendental consciousness. Afternoons and evenings, Maharishi would answer questions and teach us how to be teachers of meditation.

One of his favorite topics was the connection between modern science and Vedic science. After getting a master's degree in physics, he had studied metaphysics with one of the great swamis of India, so he could integrate both worlds. He taught us how the unified field that physics has discovered is the same as our own consciousness, that the fundamental level of the universe is the fundamental level of ourselves. And most importantly, he taught us how to experience this unity, where the duality of subject and object disappears and separation merges into oneness. This is the source of creation, a realm of bliss where even the concept of enemy doesn't exist. It's the level from which energy manifests into matter and form. Enlightened people live there all the time, but all of us can experience it, and once we do, our reality is different.

Ordinarily, our awareness is directed via sense perception outwards to physical objects. When we meditate, we reverse this direction and move our awareness back towards its source, the unified field. The mind goes inward and perceives progressively more refined levels of thinking until all thoughts drop away and we reach the ground state of transcendental consciousness, in which the mind is alert but without thoughts, pure awareness without an object. In place of thoughts, we are filled with a joy that can only be described as divine. Here we are united with all of creation. We are no longer observing the universe; we *are* the universe.

The path to transcendental consciousness, however, is not always smooth. Our stresses — the inner effects of our past actions — can make our minds murky and unsettled, thus blocking us off from a clear experience of the transcendent. But stress can be healed. During Transcendental Meditation the nervous system repairs itself and removes the obstructions so that our awareness isn't confined to the surface thinking level but can flow into the silent depths, providing deep rest for the mind and body. In this physiological condition, stress is cured and transcendental consciousness experienced.

The process can be unsettling because as stresses are dissolved, some of their qualities may affect our awareness in the form of physical pain, old buried emotions, or hectic streams of thoughts. Sometimes the unconscious has to be brought into consciousness before it can be healed.

One day during the teacher training course, I was sitting in my room wrapped in deep stillness, breathing lightly, tendrils of air curling into a vast space behind my closed eyes. My mantra had gone beyond sound to become a pulse of light in an emptiness that contained everything.

Suddenly an electric shock flashed down my spine and through my body. My head snapped back, limbs jerked, a cry burst from my throat. Every muscle in my body contracted — neck rigid, jaws clenched, forehead tight. Bolts of pain shot through me in all directions, then drew together in my chest. Heart attack! I thought. I managed to lie down, then noticed I wasn't breathing — maybe I was already dead. I groaned and gulped a huge breath, which stirred a whirl of thoughts and images.

Vietnam again: Rotor wind from a hovering helicopter flails the water of a rice paddy while farmers run frantically for cover. Points of fire spark out from a bamboo grove to become doppplered whines past my ears. A plane dives on the grove to release a bomb, which tumbles end over end and bursts into an orange globe of napalm. A man in my arms shakes in spasms as his chest gushes blood.

I held my head and tried to force the images out, but the montage of scenes flowed on, needing release. I could only lie there under a torrent of grief, regret, terror, and guilt. My chest felt like it was caving in under the pressure. I clung to my mantra like a lifeline to sanity. I was breathing in short, shallow gasps, but gradually my breath slowed and deepened, and the feelings became less gripping. I reoriented back into the present but was stunned for the rest of the afternoon.

Next day I was confused and irritable and could hardly meditate or sleep. But the following day I felt lightened and relieved, purged of a load of trauma, and my meditations were clear. My anxiety about the war was much less; the violence was in the past, not raging right now in my head.

Gradually I became aware of a delicate joy permeating not just me but also my surroundings. I knew somehow it had always been there, inhering deep in everything, but my stress had been blocking my perception of it. Rather than being confined to my small individuality, I was one with the universe, united with everything in a field of felicity. This perception faded, but it gave me a glimpse of what enlightenment must be like.

The whole experience was a dramatic example of what Maharishi called "unstressing." When the nervous system achieves the deep calm of meditation, it spontaneously heals itself and can then experience higher states of consciousness. Physiological research has shown that during TM oxygen consumption decreases twice as much as it does during deep sleep. Brain waves become more coherent, changing from the usual scattered, disordered patterns into synchronized waves coordinating across both hemispheres, an indication of more integrated mental functioning. Blood flow to the brain increases.

On the skin, electrical conductance decreases, a sign of relaxation. In the blood stream, the stress hormone cortisol decreases; serotonin, a neurotransmitter that relieves depression and promotes well being, increases; arginine vasopressin, a hormone that regulates blood pressure and improves memory and learning ability, increases; blood lactate level decreases, indicating lessened anxiety. And rather than being in a trance, the person is fully alert and aware of the surroundings. This physiological condition defines a fourth state of consciousness distinct from the three usual states of waking, dreaming, and deep sleep. In this rejuvenating transcendental consciousness, the physiology repairs the damage done by traumatic events and illnesses.

More than anything else I've experienced, Transcendental Meditation creates a peaceful inner change. The personality and basic self remain the same, but fear and hostility diminish. We become more friendly to ourselves, and so we can be more friendly to others. As our personal stresses are healed, the mind functions better and we gain access to more of our mental potential. We're more able to perceive and correct the sources of social stress that surround us.

Recent research has shown that the effects don't stop with the individual. Large groups of people meditating together produce coherence and stability not just in themselves but also in the society around them. This extended effect has been demonstrated in experiments in Massachusetts, Rhode Island, Iowa, Washington DC, New Delhi, Manila, Puerto Rico, Nicaragua, El Salvador, Iran and Holland, where large groups met for long meditations. During every assembly, crime, violence and accidents in the surrounding region dropped and the composite Quality of Life Index for public health, economics, and social harmony rose. All the changes were statistically highly significant. The groups of meditators improved the whole society: Negativity decreased, positivity increased. After the assemblies ended, the figures returned to their previous levels. The results were calculated by comparing data from different time periods to insure that the only variable was the meditation course, thus establishing it as the cause of the change.

I attended two of these assemblies, in Washington DC and Iowa, and the experiences were wonderful. Meditating with thousands of other people strengthens the results. The mental emanations reinforce one another into a palpable effect of group consciousness. I enjoyed deeper levels of inner silence and clearer infusions of transcendental energy. Outside of meditation, we treated one another with a harmony and tenderness that I'd never experienced in a group of people before. It was a taste of what an ideal society could be like.

How can meditators sitting with their eyes closed influence people many miles away? Quantum physics describes how everything in the universe is connected through underlying fields of energy. The electromagnetic field is an example. A transmitter sends waves through this invisible field, and receivers many miles away instantly convert them into sound and pictures. Similarly, our minds send mental energy through the field of consciousness that connects everyone. We are all continually transmitting and receiving these influences. The mental atmosphere we share is loaded with them, and the program they're broadcasting is frequently one of fear, frustration, anger and aggression. This toxicity is generated largely by the social and economic structures that dominate our lives. It pollutes the collective consciousness, resulting in cloudy thinking and harmful actions. All of us are affected — and infected — to some degree by this. Under this sway, persons with a heavy load of personal stress become more prone to turn to crime to solve their problems. As this negative atmosphere intensifies and the pressures mount, groups of people turn to the mass criminality of warfare.

Wars are hurricanes of the collective consciousness. Hurricanes relieve the physical atmosphere of excess heat that has built up. They result afterwards in a more balanced climatic condition, but they do that destructively. Similarly, wars relieve excess stress in the psychic atmosphere and bring a temporary peace, but their destructiveness generates more stress and another war.

In contrast to this stormy approach, a meditator in transcendental consciousness broadcasts the qualities inherent to that plane: peace, orderliness, harmony. And when many meditators reach transcendental consciousness together, their energies reinforce one another into a surge of positivity that overrides the stressful emissions of the surrounding population. The minds of everyone in the area receive this broadcast of coherence. It's a very subtle effect that is under the threshold of most people's perceptual awareness, but they are influenced through this field where all human minds are joined. This life-nurturing energy purifies the collective consciousness of fear and hostility before those negative forces can build up and erupt into crime and war.

Experiments demonstrated the effects on war. As civil war was raging in Lebanon, a group gathered nearby in Israel to practice long meditations. During their assembly, the intensity of fighting in Lebanon lessened and war deaths plummeted. In Israel, crime, traffic accidents, fires, and other indicators of social disorder decreased. All the changes were statistically highly significant.

A further experiment showed even more dramatic results. According to the ancient Vedic tradition, if a very large number of people meditate together, positive influences will occur globally. Maharishi decided to test this with seven thousand meditators, the square root of one percent of the world population. He gathered them together on the TM campus in Fairfield, Iowa, for long meditations. The results thousands of miles away in Lebanon were a seventy-one percent decrease in war deaths, a sixty-eight percent decrease in injuries, a forty-eight percent decrease in combat incidents, and a sixty-six percent increase in cooperative efforts to end the civil war. A time-series analysis of the results confirmed the causation.

Groups of seven thousand meditators also reduce terrorism. During three of these large assemblies, worldwide terrorism dropped by an average of seventy-two percent as compared to all other weeks in a two-year period, based on data compiled by the Rand Corporation. Statistical analysis ruled out the possibility that the reduction was due to cycles, trends, seasonal changes, or drifts in the measures used.

Peer-reviewed studies of these experiments have been published in the *Journal of Conflict Resolution*, *Journal of Mind and Behavior*, *Journal of Crime and Justice*, *Social Indicators Research*, and other academic publications. Twenty-three studies based on fifty experiments document the long-distance effects of large groups of meditators in reducing violence and improving quality of life.

With this overwhelming evidence Maharishi approached the governments of the world and requested that they establish these groups on a permanent basis to secure peace and social harmony.

The governments of the world weren't interested.

So Maharishi decided to build a long-term group. With the help of a wealthy donor he constructed a residential center in India and filled it with seven thousand meditators practicing several hours a day. The other experiments had been short-term, lasting a few weeks or months, but this one lasted two years — from the late '80s into the early '90s, a time that fundamentally changed the world. The Cold War ended, Communism collapsed, the people of Eastern Europe and the Soviet Union freed themselves of totalitarian rule, the Berlin Wall came down, eighty nations signed an agreement that saved the ozone layer, black and white South Africans dismantled apartheid. It was a period of unprecedented good will, a breakthrough for world peace. Former enemies signed arms reduction and nonaggression treaties; hostile borders became open and friendly.

But the donor ran out of money. He had already expended most of his fortune supporting the group and couldn't continue. Maharishi tried again to convince governments to take over the funding, an amount per year that was a fraction of what they spend on the military per one heartbeat.

Again, no government was interested. Why did they turn down such a scientifically verified program that would cost little, harm nothing, and possibly bring world peace?

In three of the countries that participated in the earlier experiments, governments were thrown out of office after the assemblies. Three dictators — the Shah in Iran, Somoza in Nicaragua, and Marcos in the Philippines — had invited the TM teachers because their populations were rising in rebellion. They hoped the meditating groups would act as a social tranquilizer that would pacify the rebels. The opposite turned out to be the case. The increased coherence generated by the groups enabled the whole society to join together and throw out the dictators with a minimum of violence. Other governments didn't want to risk losing power through a similar upsurge in the collective consciousness of their people.

Another reason was that although many governments pay lip service to peace, they don't really want it. What they want is to use the military to control their people and enforce their aggressive foreign policies. They also profit from the arms trade; peace would be bad for business.

A third reason is that the concept of meditators being able to decrease violence half a world away is just to unconventional for most politicians to comprehend. It doesn't fit the worldview they've been educated into. Our society is still living in the shadow of nineteenth-century empiricism, where matter was seen as the basis of reality. Science has moved far beyond this position, but the old view still has a lingering effect on our thinking, causing us to reject what we don't understand. The insights of unified field physics are only slowly being absorbed by the general population. Most people can't yet comprehend that energy rather than matter is the basic component of the universe, and that this energy is identical with our own consciousness.

In addition, the intellectual rebellion against dogmatic religion has gone to the opposite extreme where many people now embrace skepticism as the ultimate wisdom. Doubt has become the new orthodoxy, and definitive statements about the world are automatically suspect.

Seeing consciousness as primary and matter as being its manifestation is a whole different way of looking at the universe and will require some getting used to. But every paradigm shift in human thinking has had to confront the prejudices of its time. As Arthur Schopenhauer said, a new worldview is first ridiculed, then attacked, and finally accepted as self-evident.

But unfortunately, in the early 1990s when the group of seven thousand meditators had to be dissolved, negative consequences followed swiftly: The USA decided for full-spectrum dominance and developed new nuclear weapons; The first Gulf War broke out; Yugoslavia dissolved into violent chaos; terrorism multiplied. Destructive trends in all areas of life continue to engulf us.

Maharishi didn't give up. He started rebuilding the group on his own. To finance it, he raised the prices for learning TM and for his ayurvedic health programs. Though Mararishi died in 2008, by 2010 there were groups of four thousand in India and two thousand in Iowa, both of them growing. If the number of meditators continues to increase, we could all be in for a new era.

Scientific evidence indicates this technique can cure the root cause of war — stress in the collective consciousness — and bring world peace. This could be the most important discovery of our time, and we can all participate in it. Several studies have shown that individuals meditating on their own for twenty minutes twice a day also contribute to this effect. More information and citations on the research can be found at www.permanentpeace.org.

Together we can end war! We must!

Peace, Salaam, Shalom, Shantih.

The True Story of the Bilderberg Group

By Daniel Estulin

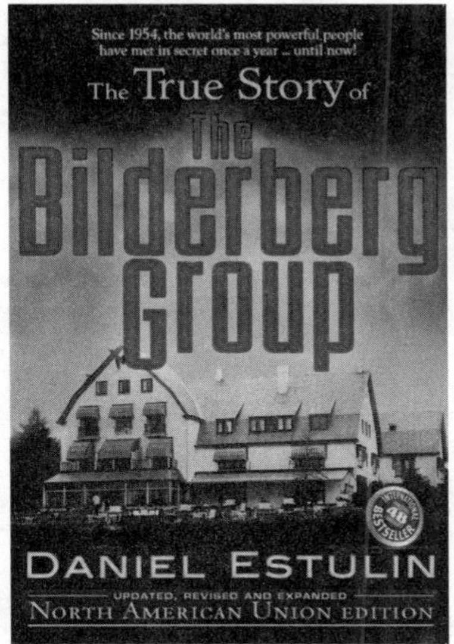

Since 1954, the world's most powerful people have met in secret once a year ... until now!
The True Story of The Bilderberg Group
Daniel Estulin
Updated, Revised and Expanded
North American Union Edition

More than a center of influence, the Bilderberg Group is a shadow world government, hatching plans of domination at annual meetings ... and under a cone of media silence.

THE TRUE STORY OF THE BILDERBERG GROUP goes inside the secret meetings and sheds light on why a group of politicians, businessmen, bankers and other mighty individuals formed the world's most powerful society. As Benjamin Disraeli, one of England's greatest Prime Ministers, noted, "The world is governed by very different personages from what is imagined by those who are not behind the scenes."

Included are unpublished and never-before-seen photographs and other documentation of meetings, as this riveting account exposes the past, present and future plans of the Bilderberg elite.

Softcover: **$24.95** (ISBN: 9780979988622) • 432 pages • Size: 6 x 9

Dr. Mary's Monkey

How the Unsolved Murder of a Doctor, a Secret Laboratory in New Orleans and Cancer-Causing Monkey Viruses are Linked to Lee Harvey Oswald, the JFK Assassination and Emerging Global Epidemics

By Edward T. Haslam, Foreword by Jim Marrs

Evidence of top-secret medical experiments and cover-ups of clinical blunders

The 1964 murder of a nationally known cancer researcher sets the stage for this gripping exposé of medical professionals enmeshed in covert government operations over the course of three decades. Following a trail of police records, FBI files, cancer statistics, and medical journals, this revealing book presents evidence of a web of medical secret-keeping that began with the handling of evidence in the JFK assassination and continued apace, sweeping doctors into cover-ups of cancer outbreaks, contaminated polio vaccine, the genesis of the AIDS virus, and biological weapon research using infected monkeys.

Softcover: **$19.95** (ISBN: 0977795306) • 320 pages • Size: 5 1/2 x 8 1/2

The Franklin Scandal

A Story of Powerbrokers, Child Abuse & Betrayal

BY NICK BRYANT

A chilling exposé of corporate corruption and government cover-ups, this account of a nationwide child-trafficking and pedophilia ring tells a sordid tale of corruption in high places. The scandal originally surfaced during an investigation into Omaha, Nebraska's failed Franklin Federal Credit Union and took the author beyond the Midwest and ultimately to Washington, DC. Implicating businessmen, senators, major media corporations, the CIA, and even the venerable Boys Town organization, this extensively researched report includes firsthand interviews with key witnesses and explores a controversy that has received scant media attention.

The Franklin Scandal is the story of a underground ring that pandered children to a cabal of the rich and powerful. The ring's pimps were a pair of Republican powerbrokers who used Boys Town as a pedophiliac reservoir, and had access to the highest levels of our government and connections to the CIA.

Nick Bryant is a journalist whose work largely focuses on the plight of disadvantaged children in the United States. His mainstream and investigative journalism has been featured in *Gear, Playboy, The Reader*, and on Salon.com. He is the coauthor of *America's Children: Triumph of Tragedy*. He lives in New York City.

Hardcover: **$24.95** (ISBN: 0977795357) • 676 pages

The Oil Card

Global Economic Warfare in the 21st Century

BY JAMES NORMAN

Challenging the conventional wisdom surrounding high oil prices, this compelling argument sheds an entirely new light on free-market industry fundamentals.

By deciphering past, present, and future geopolitical events, it makes the case that oil pricing and availability have a long history of being employed as economic weapons by the United States. Despite ample world supplies and reserves, high prices are now being used to try to rein in China — a reverse of the low-price strategy used in the 1980s to deprive the Soviets of hard currency. Far from conspiracy theory, the debate notes how the US has previously used the oil majors, the Saudis, and market intervention to move markets — and shows how this is happening again.

Softcover **$14.95** (ISBN 0977795390) • 288 PAGES • Size: 5.5 x 8.5

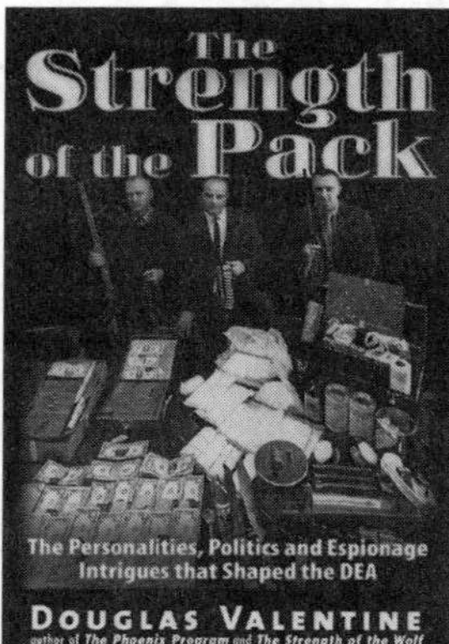

The Strength of the Pack

The Personalities, Politics and Espionage Intrigues that Shaped the DEA

BY DOUG VALENTINE

Through interviews with former narcotics agents, politicians, and bureaucrats, this exposé documents previously unknown aspects of the history of federal drug law enforcement from the formation of the Bureau of Narcotics and Dangerous Drugs and the creation of the Drug Enforcement Administration (DEA) up until the present day. Written in an easily accessible style, the narrative examines how successive administrations expanded federal drug law enforcement operations at home and abroad; investigates how the CIA comprised the war on drugs; analyzes the Reagan, Bush, and Clinton administrations' failed attempts to alter the DEA's course; and traces the agency's evolution into its final and current stage of "narco-terrorism."

Douglas Valentine is a former private investigator and consultant and the author of *The Hotel Tacloban, The Phoenix Program, The Strength of the Wolf*, and *TDY*.

Softcover: **$24.95** (ISBN: 9780979988653) • 480 pages • Size: 6 x 9

Perfectibilists

The 18th Century Bavarian Illuminati

by Terry Melanson

The shadowy Illuminati grace many pages of fiction as the sinister all-powerful group pulling the strings behind the scenes, but very little has been printed in English about the actual Enlightenment-era secret society, its activities, its members, and its legacy ... until now.

First choosing the name Perfectibilists, their enigmatic leader Adam Weishaupt soon thought that sounded too bizarre and changed it to the Order of the Illuminati.

Presenting an authoritative perspective, this definitive study chronicles the rise and fall of the fabled Illuminati, revealing their methods of infiltrating governments and education systems, and their blueprint for a successful cabal, which echoes directly forward through groups like the Order of Skull & Bones to our own era.

Featuring biographies of more than 400 confirmed members and copiously illustrated, this book brings light to a 200-year-old mystery.

Softcover: **$19.95** (ISBN: 9780977795381) • 530 pages • Size: 6 x 9

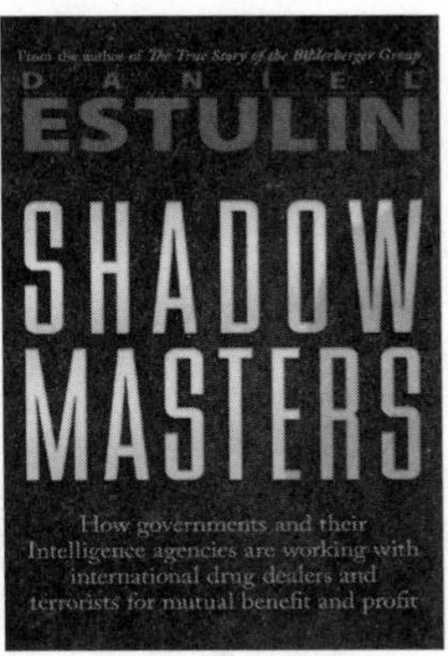

ShadowMasters

by Daniel Estulin

An International Network of Governments and Secret-Service Agencies Working Together with Drug Dealers and Terrorists for Mutual Benefit and Profit

This investigation examines how behind-the-scenes collaboration between government, intelligence services, and drug traffickers has lined the pockets of big business and Western banks. Among the examples cited are the cozy relationship between Victor Bout, the largest weaponry dealer in the world, and George Bush's administration; the NGOs who are plundering Darfur with the help of big multinationals seeking to take over the oilfields around the country; the ties that the Muslim Brotherhood maintains with the White House despite their involvement with the March 11th attacks in Madrid; and the embezzlement of more than $2.8 million from the International Monetary Fund by Roman Abramovich, the biggest oligarch in Russia.

Daniel Estulin is an award-winning investigative journalist and author of *The True Story of the Bilderberg Group*.

Softcover: **$24.95** (ISBN: 9780979988615) • 432 pages • Size: 6 x 9

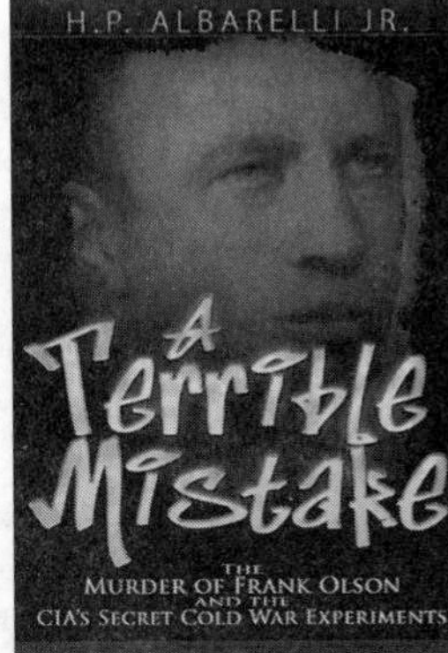

A Terrible Mistake

The Murder of Frank Olson and the CIA's Secret Cold War Experiments

by H.P. Albarelli Jr.

In his nearly 10 years of research into the death of Dr. Frank Olson, writer and investigative journalist H.P. Albarelli Jr. gained unique and unprecedented access to many former CIA, FBI, and Federal Narcotics Bureau officials, including several who actually oversaw the CIA's mind- control programs from the 1950s to the early 1970s.

A Terrible Mistake takes readers into a frequently bizarre and always frightening world, colored and dominated by Cold War concerns and fears. For the past 30 years the death of biochemist Frank Olson has ranked high on the nation's list of unsolved and perplexing mysteries. *A Terrible Mistake* solves the mystery and reveals in shocking detail the identities of Olson's murderers. The book also takes readers into the strange world of government mind-control programs and close collaboration with the Mafia.

H. P. Albarelli Jr. is an investigative journalist whose work has appeared in numerous publications and newspapers across the nation and is the author of the novel *The Heap*. He lives in Tampa, Florida.

Hardcover • $34.95 ISBN 978-0977795376 • 912 pages

Expendable Elite

One Soldier's Journey into Covert Warfare

BY DANIEL MARVIN , FOREWORD BY MARTHA RAYE

A special operations perspective on the Viet Nam War and the truth about a White House concerned with popular opinion

This true story of a special forces officer in Viet Nam in the mid-1960s exposes the unique nature of the elite fighting force and how covert operations are developed and often masked to permit — and even sponsor — assassination, outright purposeful killing of innocents, illegal use of force, and bizarre methods in combat operations. *Expendable Elite* reveals the fear that these warriors share with no other military person: not fear of the enemy they have been trained to fight in battle, but fear of the wrath of the US government should they find themselves classified as "expendable." This book centers on the CIA mission to assassinate Cambodian Crown Prince Nordum Sihanouk, the author's unilateral aborting of the mission, the CIA's dispatch of an ARVN regiment to attack and destroy the camp and kill every person in it as retribution for defying the agency, and the dramatic rescue of eight American Green Berets and hundreds of South Viet Namese.

— NEW SPECIAL VICTORY EDITION — Commemorating our Free Speech Federal Court triumph that allows you to read this book exposing the true ways of war!

— READ THE BOOK, "THEY" DON'T WANT YOU TO! —

DANIEL MARVIN is a retired Lieutenant Colonel in the US Army Special Forces and former Green Beret.

Softcover: **$19.95** (ISBN 0977795314) • 420 pages • 150+ photos & maps

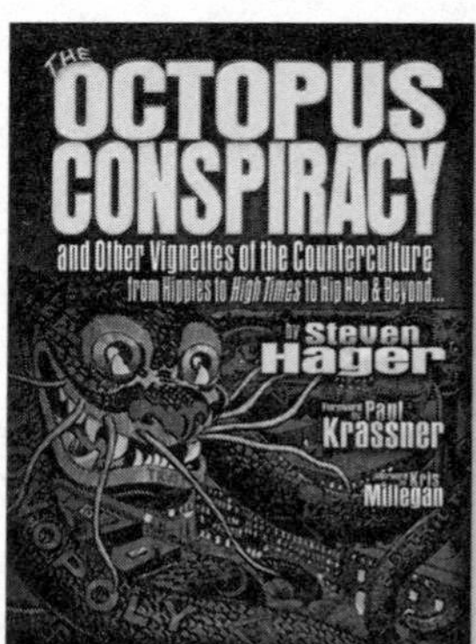

The Octopus Conspiracy

and Other Vignettes of the Counterculture from Hippies to High Times to Hip Hop and Beyond ...

BY STEVEN HAGER

Insightful essays on the genesis of subcultures from new wave and yuppies to graffiti and rap.

From the birth of hip-hop culture in the South Bronx to the influence of nightclubs in shaping the modern art world in New York, a generation of countercultural events and icons are brought to life in this personal account of the life and experiences of a former investigative reporter and editor of High Times. Evidence from cutting-edge conspiracy research including the real story behind the JFK assassination and the Franklin Savings and Loan cover-up is presented. Quirky personalities and compelling snapshots of life in the 1980s and 1990s emerge in this collection of vignettes from a landmark figure in journalism.

STEVEN HAGER is the author of ***Adventures in Counterculture, Art After Midnight,*** and ***Hip Hop.*** He is a former reporter for the New York Daily News and an editor of ***High Times.***

Hardcover: **$19.95** (ISBN 0975290614) • 320 pages • Size: 6 x 9

Fixing America

Breaking the Strangehold of Corporate Rule, Big Media, and the Religious Right

BY JOHN BUCHANAN, FOREWORD BY JOHN MCCONNELL

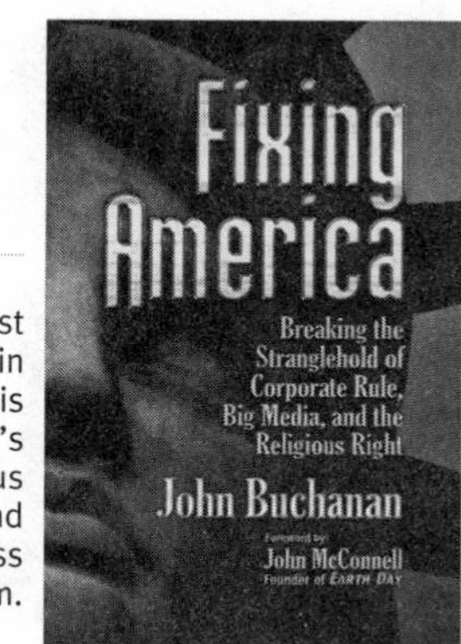

An explosive analysis of what ails the United States

An award-winning investigative reporter provides a clear, honest diagnosis of corporate rule, big media, and the religious right in this damning analysis. Exposing the darker side of capitalism, this critique raises alarms about the security of democracy in today's society, including the rise of the corporate state, the insidious role of professional lobbyists, the emergence of religion and theocracy as a right-wing political tactic, the failure of the mass media, and the sinister presence of an Orwellian neo-fascism.

Softcover: **$19.95**, (ISBN 0-975290681) 216 Pages, 5.5 x 8.5

The 9/11 Mystery Plane

And the Vanishing of America

by Mark Gaffney

Foreword by

Dr. David Ray Griffin

Unlike other accounts of the historic attacks on 9/11, this discussion surveys the role of the world's most advanced military command and control plane, the E-4B, in the day's events and proposes that the horrific incidents were the work of a covert operation staged within elements of the US military and the intelligence community. Presenting hard evidence, the account places the world's most advanced electronics platform circling over the White House at approximately the time of the Pentagon attack. The argument offers an analysis of the new evidence within the context of the events and shows that it is irreconcilable with the official 9/11 narrative.

Mark H. Gaffney is an environmentalist, a peace activist, a researcher, and the author of *Dimona, the Third Temple?;* and *Gnostic Secrets of the Naassenes*. He lives in Chiloquin, Oregon. Dr. David Ray Griffin is a professor emeritus at the Claremont School of Theology, and the author of *The 9/11 Commission Report: Omissions and Distortions*, and *The New Pearl Harbor*. He lives in Santa Barbara, California.

Softcover • $19.95 • ISBN 9780979988608 • 336 Pages

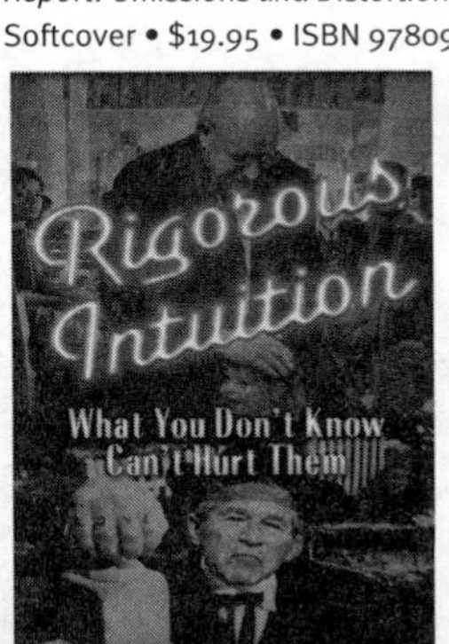

Rigorous Intuition

What You Don't Know, Can't Hurt Them

by Jeff Wells

"In Jeff's hands, tinfoil hats become crowns and helmets of the purest gold. I strongly suggest that you all pay attention to what he has to say." —Arthur Gilroy, Booman Tribune

A welcome source of analysis and commentary for those prepared to go deeper — and darker — than even most alternative media permit, this collection from one of the most popular conspiracy theory arguments on the internet will assist readers in clarifying their own arguments and recognizing disinformation. Tackling many of the most difficult subjects that define our time — including 9/11, the JonBenet Ramsey case, and "High Weirdness" — these studies, containing the best of the Rigorous Intuition blog as well as original content, make connections that both describe the current, alarming predicament and suggest a strategy for taking back the world. Following the maxim "What you don't know can't hurt them," this assortment of essays and tools, including the updated and expanded "Coincidence Theorists' Guide to 9/11," guides the intellectually curious down further avenues of study and scrutiny and helps readers feel empowered rather than vulnerable.

Jeff Wells is the author of the novel *Anxious Gravity*. He lives in Toronto, Ontario.

Softcover • $19.95 • 978-0-9777953-2-1 • 505 Pages

Fighting For G.O.D. ***(Gold, Oil, Drugs)***

by Jeremy Begin, Art by Laureen Salk

This racehorse tour of American history and current affairs scrutinizes key events transcending the commonly accepted liberal/conservative political ideologies — in a large-size comic-book format.

This analysis delves into aspects of the larger framework into which 9/11 fits and scrutinizes the ancestry of the players who transcend commonly accepted liberal/conservative political ideologies. This comic-book format analysis examines the Neo Con agenda and its relationship to "The New World Order. This book discusses key issues confronting America's citizenry and steps the populace can take to not only halt but reverse the march towards totalitarianism.

Jeremy Begin is a long-time activist/organizer currently residing in California's Bay Area. Lauren Salk is an illustrator living in Boston.

Softcover: **$9.95**, (ISBN 0977795330) 64 Pages, 8.5 x 11

Upcoming Releases

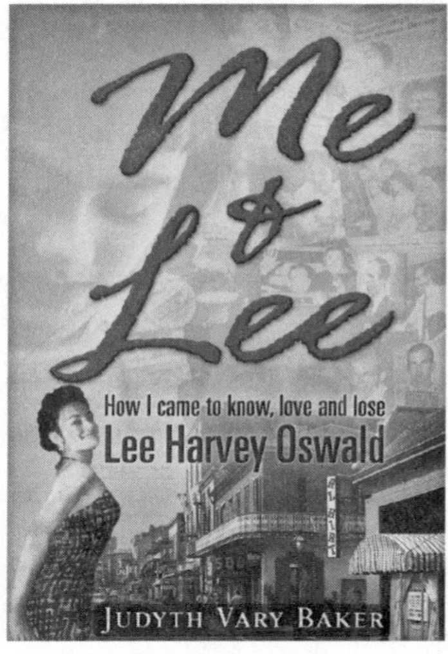

Me & Lee

How I Came to Know, Love and Lose Lee Harvey Oswald

by Judyth Vary Baker

Foreword by

Edward T. Haslam

Judyth Vary was once a promising science student who dreamed of finding a cure for cancer; this exposé is her account of how she strayed from a path of mainstream scholarship at the University of Florida to a life of espionage in New Orleans with Lee Harvey Oswald. In her narrative she offers extensive documentation on how she came to be a cancer expert at such a young age, the personalities who urged her to relocate to New Orleans, and what lead to her involvement in the development of a biological weapon that Oswald was to smuggle into Cuba to eliminate Fidel Castro. Details on what she knew of Kennedy's impending assassination, her conversations with Oswald as late as two days before the killing, and her belief that Oswald was a deep-cover intelligence agent who was framed for an assassination he was actually trying to prevent, are also revealed.

Judyth Vary Baker is a former teacher, and artist. Edward T. Haslam is the author of *Dr. Mary's Monkey*. He lives in Florida.

Hardcover • $24.95 • ISBN 9780979988677 • 480 Pages

1-800-556-2012

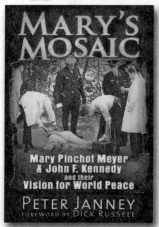

Mary's Mosaic

Mary Pinchot Meyer & John F. Kennedy and their Vision for World Peace

by Peter Janney

Foreword by Dick Russell

Challenging the conventional wisdom surrounding the murder of Mary Pinchot Meyer, this exposé offers new information and evidence that individuals within the upper echelons of the CIA were not only involved in the assassination of President John F. Kennedy, but her demise as well. Written by the son of a CIA lifer and a college classmate of Mary Pinchot Meyer, this insider's story examines how Mary used events and circumstances in her personal life to become an acolyte for world peace. The most famous convert to her philosophy was reportedly President John F. Kennedy, with whom she was said to have begun a serious love relationship in January 1962. Offering an insightful look into the era and its culture, the narrative sheds light on how in the wake of the Cuban Missile Crisis, she helped the president realize that a Cold War mentality was of no use and that the province of world peace was the only worthwhile calling. Details on her experiences with LSD, its influences on her and Kennedy's thinking, his attempts to negotiate a limited nuclear test ban treaty with Soviet Premier Nikita Khrushchev, and to find lasting peace with Fidel Castro are also included.

Peter Janney is a former psychologist and naturopathic healer and a cofounder of the American Mental Health Alliance. He was one of the first graduates of the MIT Sloan School of Management's Entrepreneurship Skills Transfer Program. He lives in Beverly, Massachusetts. Dick Russell is the author of *Black Genius: And the American Experience*, *Eye of the Whale*, *The Man Who Knew Too Much*, and *Striper Wars: An American Fish Story*. He is a former staff writer for *TV Guide* magazine, a staff reporter for *Sports Illustrated*, and has contributed numerous articles to publications ranging from *Family Health* to the *Village Voice*. He lives in Boston, Massachusetts and Los Angeles.

Hardcover • $24.95 • ISBN 978-0-9799886-3-9 • 480 Pages

Upcoming Releases

The King of Nepal

Life Before the Drug Wars

by Joseph R. Pietri

From the halcyon days of easily accessible drugs to years of government intervention and a surging black market, this tale chronicles a former drug smuggler's 50-year career in the drug trade, its evolution into a multibillion-dollar business, and the characters he met along the way. The journey begins with the infamous Hippie Hash trail that led from London and Amsterdam overland to Nepal where, prior to the early1970s, hashish was legal and smoked freely in Nepal, India, Afghanistan, and Laos; marijuana and opium were sold openly in Hindu temples in India and much of Asia; and cannabis was widely cultivated in Nepal and Afghanistan for use in food, medicine, and cloth.

In documenting the stark contrasts of the ensuing years, the narrative examines the impact of the financial incentives awarded by international institutions such as the U.S. government to outlaw the cultivation of cannabis in Nepal and Afghanistan and to make hashish and opium illegal in Turkey—the demise of the U.S. "good old boy" dope network, the eruption of a violent criminal society, and the birth of a global black market for hard drugs—as well as the schemes smugglers employed to get around customs agents and various regulations.J

Joseph R. Pietri is a former drug smuggler who is now a legal purveyor of cannabis for medicinal purposes.

Softcover • $19.95 • ISBN 978-097998866 • 336 Pages

The Last Circle

Danny Casalaro's Investigation into The Octopus and the Promis Software Scandal

byCheri Seymour

The Last Circle is an unparalleled investigation into one of the most organized and complex criminal enterprises that American has ever seen.

Investigative reporter Cheri Seymour spent 18 years following the trail of the Octopus, probing the behind-the-scenes dynamics of a labyrinth that encompassed multiple covert operations involving a maze of politicians; NSC, CIA, and DOJ officials; organized crime figures; intelligence agents; arms sales; drug-trafficking; high-tech money laundering; and the death of Washington D.C. journalist Danny Casolaro.

Through law enforcement agencies as far-ranging as the FBI, U.S. Customs, police and sheriff's departments, and even the RCMP national security division, Seymour learned that the official head of the Octopus resided in the U.S. Department of Justice, supported by an out-of-control presidential administration, its tentacles comprised of a cabal of "Old Boy" cronies, true believers, who held that the end justified the means.

They gave corruption a new meaning as they stampeded through the Constitution, cowboyed the intelligence community, blazed new trails into drug cartels and organized crime, while simultaneously growing new tentacles that reached into every facet of criminal enterprise. The theft of high-tech software (PROMIS) for use in money-laundering and espionage; illegal drug and arms trafficking in Latin America; and exploitation of sovereign Indian nations were just a few of these enterprises.

The Last Circle educates and inspires because it proves that an average citizen can make a difference in exposing and bringing to justice high-level criminals. For readers who like mystery and intrigue, it is an interesting first-person account of a female sleuth's journey through the nation's most hidden criminal underworld.

Softcover • $24.95 • ISBN 978-1936296002 • 480 Pages